By: CRAIG SULLIVAN

BREAKING WIND

Llumina
Press

ISBN: 978-1-62550-306-0 (PB)
       978-1-60594-941-3 (HC)
       978-1-60594-867-6 (Ebook)

Printed in the United States of America by Llumina Press

Library of Congress Control Number: 2011962266

BREAKING WIND

PROLOGUE

"**M**r. Letterman... Mr. Letterman, are you here? Nubert Letterman, please respond when your name is called." Miss Crabtree stood before the class, her cardigan sweater buttoned high emphasizing her stiff, authoritarian stature. She ran her long finger down the attendance list, checking it twice, knowing full well Nubert Letterman was in attendance.

Nub continued to stare out of the classroom window without looking up or acknowledging the plea.

"Mr. Letterman, why do we have to go through this routine every day? Just say present, *please.*"

Jocelyn Steed, pin curls darting here and there as she shook her head in disbelief, leaned forward from her position directly behind Nub in the 'S' row, and gave his chair a stout kick causing the chair legs to screech on the tile floor.

Nub jumped to attention, looking around the room at all of the other fifth graders staring at him. "What?"

Jocelyn leaned forward and whispered while Crabtree maneuvered her way down the aisle. "Will you just say present, *nerdo,* so we can get this over with? Jeez, Nub, wake up."

Crabtree, reading glasses still perched on her pointy nose, made eye contact with each child she passed, expressing her stern dissatisfaction with the interruption.

Some said Nub had attention deficit disorder, others said he just could not fit in with the other kids and should be in the special-needs class. Even more said growing up on a hog farm around all that manure had stunted his social skills and maybe his brain function. Miss Crabtree just thought he was a pain in the ass.

She approached, expecting Nub to cower, but rather found further insolence as he watched a captured wooly worm slowly inch its way up his arm. "That's it, I can't take this anymore. Nubert, get out of that seat and come with me." Crabtree stood in front of Nub, bending over with her hands on her hips and her lips puckered like she had just sucked on a rotten lemon. "You are going to the office and have a talk with Principal Peters."

A rush of air was sucked out of the room as every kid held his breath. Going to the office at the hands of Miss Crabtree was a sure-fire way to get the dreaded paddle, what appeared to a fifth grader to be a baseball-bat-sized flat board made of sturdy oak, splintered with battle scars from juvenile delinquents of prior years. The flat lands of the Midwest had yet to be burdened with the liberal rules that outlawed corporal punishment. And Principal Peters still believed in not sparing the rod, much to Miss Crabtree's pleasure.

Miss Crabtree's heels clicked on the terrazzo hall floor as she humped her way to the office, stopping every ten steps and summoning Nub to "Step to it, there's no use crying about it now," even though Nub wasn't crying, much to her dismay.

She turned and marched off again as Nub ambled along slowly, hoping the five pairs of underwear he had systematically layered didn't slide down and cause his wrinkled pants to look unusually bunched. As he passed an unoccupied classroom door, he daintily placed the wooly worm on the door handle, and continued his slow pace toward the school office.

What Crabtree didn't realize, or contemplate, was that there was a pretty detailed plan in place.

Nub had decided the night before to sacrifice himself in the name of science, as opposed to sitting all day listening to a boring teacher regurgitate outdated facts from a ten-year-old textbook. He spent most of the evening in a computer chat room, originating at MIT in Boston, discussing a programming methodology that could decipher code used by satellite television receivers. In other words, he was on the verge of circumventing the scramble used to prevent pirating the best TV channels. It was worth the sacrifice, as long as his underwear strategy proved effective, and Principal Peters saw it necessary to send him home after issuing the penal justice.

"You just sit yourself down right there," Miss Crabtree commanded, pointing her long finger, with a well-manicured half-inch nail, at an unpadded oak chair across from the office counter, separating the uneducated from the educated.

Crabtree looked at the school secretary, who was busying herself picking lint off of her cashmere sweater, and said, "I've got Nubert here again. I do not want him back in my classroom until he learns some manners. I hope that is understood." She raised her voice enough to assure Principal Peters, sitting in the adjacent office, could hear her complaint.

Crabtree continued her standoff with Nub while waiting for Principal Peters, assuming he was busy with important administrative duties.

On the other side of the interior office door, Peters was excising the cover page of the latest edition of the *Sports Illustrated* swimsuit issue to be framed and placed alongside the complete collection in his home-basement man cave.

While Crabtree stood just outside the swinging office rail divider, hands on her wide hips and tapping her heeled shoe, glaring at Nub, Peters removed the magazine from his desk, slowly rose from his leather reclining chair, and walked to the doorway to observe the evolving drama.

She gave a curt glance at Peters and said, "I have twenty-four other children excited about the opportunity to engage in a discussion about the Oregon Trail ...and now probably tearing my classroom apart," she added, turning and pointing her long finger at Nub, "and one that insists on flagrant disregard of classroom authority."

"All right, Mary, this isn't boot camp, they are fifth graders. Let's calm down and I'll talk to Nub." Peters sighed and pulled at this pants, sucking in his gut. "You know as well as I do, there are some special circumstances here."

Miss Crabtree turned and stomped out of the office door, adding, "Special, my butt."

The office secretary, elbows positioned on her neat, uncluttered desk and concentrating on efficiently filing her nails, glanced at Peters. "Don't forget, Superintendent Smithy will be here," she looked up at the clock above the door, "in about fifteen minutes. The coffee is ready and the Danish is on the way up from the cafeteria." She returned to her studious chore.

Peters turned and went back into his office. Now he would have to sit across from some snot-nosed kid and try to explain the disciplinary code for picking one's nose, or whatever Crabtree found fault with on this miserable morning.

The challenge of playing mental chess with a ten-year-old was all part of the principal's job as described in every elementary school principal's handbook. Let the child sit and think about the consequences of his actions, imagining the tortuous physical harm that was to come. Of course, Nub seemed to enjoy the duel, almost as if he were challenging the intellectual and physical superiority of the teachers and administrators. Even worse, was the stigma of the special-needs child and the special care required as outlined by all of the psychologists in the *Elementary Teacher's Monthly Journal*. What a bunch of boloney. He had seen this kid in action, forging documents to skip school, getting an A on all his exams, which had to be some kind of cheating scam, and consistently out-maneuvering him when it came to discipline.

The last test of authority verses juvenile wits resulted in, what Peters considered, a draw. Nub had been given homework that included writing down the fifty-two most- used prepositions, as outlined in the *Middle School Living With Language* textbook, and using each one in a sentence. On the day the assignment was due, Nub advised Miss Crabtree that he felt the assignment was a waste of his time and good paper. Nub was marched to the principal's office for disciplinary measures commensurate with disobeying a homework assignment.

Prior to dispensing the punishment, Nub asked Principal Peters if *he* could recite all fifty-two most used prepositions. Peters responded that he certainly could, because he had completed all of his homework assignments when he was in fifth grade. Nub said, "Well then, let's hear 'em." When Peters refused to submit to the demands of a ten-year-old, Nub recited all fifty-two in alphabetical order. And then asked, "If I already know 'em, what's the use of wasting time writing them all down and using them in a sentence?"

Peters sent Nub back to class without his due punishment, but rather with advice that he try to mollify Miss Crabtree by doing what she asked, even if it did seem below his intellectual acumen.

Peters twiddled his thumbs behind his office door while Nub sat stoically, occasionally picking at his underwear that, due to the abundance of layers, was riding up his crotch something fearful. The clock above the door ticked with annoying rhythmic accuracy and the school secretary sat staring at him with a smirk that could send chills down the back of a gorilla.

Peters finally stepped out of his office, put his hands on his hips, curled his lips into a severe frown, and gave Nub a grave look of disappointment, hoping it would penetrate his nonchalant attitude. Just as Peters opened his mouth to invite Nub into the den of perpetual child abuse, Superintendent Smithy strolled through the office door, smiling as though he were starring in a toothpaste commercial. He reveled in his new position of authority as school superintendent, having recently been promoted from his prior position as Hinkley High School principal. The prior superintendent had suddenly resigned after some students used a cell phone to video him exiting a strip club in Cougar Falls. The fact that he frequented the club probably wasn't the primary motivation for his resignation as much as the continued action as he walked around the back of the building arm in arm with Barbara Boobalicious.

Superintendent Jerry Smithy was short with a paunch hanging over his belt offering a fitting ledge for his clip-on tie, mostly bald with puffs of silver hair over each ear, and since being named superintendent, wore trendy glasses on the end of his robust red nose along with a new mail-order suit.

Smithy didn't acknowledge Peters standing at the office counter, but rather went directly to the school secretary's desk. "Helen, you look lovely this morning. Have you done something with your hair? I think so...don't you lie to me." He put his finger to his chin as if contemplating a complex equation. "You look, I'd say ten years younger, if that's possible. That would make you, what, almost a teenager."

Helen blushed and pumped up her chest a little. "Oh, thank you, Jerr—," She glanced at Peters before correcting, "Mr. Smithy." She pushed at her stiff, bottle blonde curls, fluffing them. "I did have a stylist over in the Falls make some changes. It's so hard to find anyone to do, you know, current trends in Hinkley."

"Well, you sure did get trendy, I'll say that." Smithy gave another generous smile, tilted his head and looked over his glasses for one more peek at Helen's low cut sweater and then turned to Peters. "Well, Ron, everything going smoothly over here?" He looked at Nub sitting in the stiff oak chair. "What's the problem here, we got a sick one or something?" Smithy's bushy eyebrows were half absorbed into his furled forehead as he turned serious, moved closer to Peters and whispered, "Isn't that the Letterman kid, the one they think is the, uh, what do they call it, a croissant?"

Peters gave Smithy a puzzled look. He thinks the kid's a dinner roll? Peters thought a second and then cupped his hand next to his mouth and whispered back, "You mean Savant, Idiot Savant Syndrome?"

"Oh yeah, that thing. That what he's got?" Smithy said, adjusting his suit coat and straightening his tie, like the serious conversation required his attention.

"Well, I don't know. Right now he's here because Mary Crabtree didn't like his attitude."

A smile drew across Smithy's face, replacing the concerned smirk when he heard Mary's name. "How is old Mary anyway? She still like to have that martini every night? Never did figure why she couldn't find anyone. Damn good looking, just a sour disposition. I suppose that's it, no matter how good the tail is, sometimes it's the mouth that gets 'em in trouble."

Peters glanced at his secretary, hoping she couldn't hear the whispers.

"Well, we better have a look at those budget numbers. Did Helen get us any of that Danish?" Smithy turned and sauntered into Peters' office.

Peters looked at Nub and then at Smithy's back, realizing a conflict now existed. He rubbed his forehead in thought, and then approached Nub, stopping at the office rail. He straightened up and tried to look stern, pulling in his chin and giving a concerned squint. "Nub, I don't have time for you today, but I want you to remember these words. If I see you in this office again, I'll fan your butt something awful, are we clear? Now, you get out of here, and do not, do you hear me, do not cause any more trouble. Now get."

Nub slowly stood as Peters turned and walked briskly into his office and closed the door.

The secretary was on the phone urging the cafeteria personnel to send up the Danish, so Nub walked out into the hall, reviewing in his head the admonition just received from Principal Peters. Don't cause any more trouble; don't get sent back to the office. No place in that speech did he say go back to the classroom. Nub smiled and headed for the front steps of the school building.

CHAPTER 1

Ray Lightfeather leaned against the wall in a darkened corner of the Hinkley High School auditorium, watching the assemblage of local residents greet each other in muffled tones and choose their seats. Ray had his Stetson pulled down low on his forehead, making it easy to avoid any personal eye contact. There were occasional greetings directed toward him from familiar faces, Ray giving a slight nod, but no verbal response.

An ad in the twice weekly Hinkley *Messenger* announcing the meeting was vague about the purpose, but the hook, which caught Ray's attention, was the bold line; **Learn how to avoid ever paying another electric bill**, along with the offer of a buy one, get one free dinner coupon from the Kountry Kitchen Diner. Ray wasn't much concerned about his power bill, or the coupon, but he could smell a well-played scam better than most, and it perked his interest. If there was easy money about to be dispensed, it was worth his time to listen and learn.

Ray recognized two of the people seated at the table positioned center stage at the front of the auditorium. Martha Redman, secretary for the Parent Teachers Association, sat at one end, twiddling the red curls in her hair, apparently waiting for the meeting to be called to order. On the other end of the table sat Harold Hanover, hardware store owner and President of the Hinkley County Chamber of Commerce. It looked like he was the chosen moderator for the meeting. Ray couldn't place the guy sitting between them, but his well-manicured appearance, starched shirt, and pressed pants were evidence enough that he was not from Hinkley.

Harold Hanover, owner of Hanover Hardware, was well known in the county and Ray had patronized his store on occasion. At one time, Ray had offered to put a fake totem pole in Harold's store and display some authentic American Indian relics that were made in China, but Harold declined, so Ray hadn't been in the store for a while.

1

Harold had a lofty attitude of superiority and that bothered Ray. Harold felt he had a gift; even more than a gift; a God-given talent to lead those who needed led, which in Ray's opinion, was bogus. But Harold dressed the part, wearing a light gray western suit with one of those skinny string bow ties, like the early country western singers wore on Saturday night. It had little silver tips on the ends matching the silver tips on his shirt collar.

Ray reached into the hidden pocket of his leather vest and pulled out a hunk of beef jerky, getting comfortable in preparation for the start of the meeting.

◆　◆　◆

Hanover reached to the middle of the table and scooted the lone microphone to a position directly in front of his face and said, "Test, one, two, three." The archaic sound system squealed with feedback, causing everyone in the audience to cover their ears. He soundly smacked the head of the microphone, hoping to ease the ear-piercing shriek but only exacerbated the situation by adding a loud thump to the chorus of squealing electrons that now echoed off the walls of the big room.

Hanover stood to search for the school custodian for some assistance and the squeal abruptly stopped. He smiled at the waiting crowd and sat back down, leaning toward the microphone. The feedback started again only louder. Harold noticed his inner ear hearing device was screaming with the same voracity as the hall's amplification system, irritating what was already a nearly useless right ear. He pushed himself back from the microphone and plucked the hearing aid from his ear and shoved it into his pocket. The squelch silenced, and a moan of relief enveloped the crowd.

In a town as small as Hinkley, everyone knew of Harold's plight dealing with a hearing disability and also lack of sight in his right eye. Over twenty years ago he was involved in an unfortunate automobile accident with his wife while spending a pleasant Sunday afternoon looking at fall foliage.

On that fateful afternoon, Harold and his wife Edna were traveling through the Olatagwa State Forest. Edna was driving while they conversed about different things and observed the iridescent fall colors shimmering in the afternoon sunlight. Harold was telling Edna about his most recent encounter with Murt Featherstone in their hardware store, haggling over the price of a garden spade. Harold ended the story about Murt, saying, "Boy, she's the biggest bitch in Hinkley County." Then he thought for a moment and looking out the window muttered, "Well, the second biggest."

That was where the facts of the story got a little murky, at least as far as the Hinkley County Sheriff Reginald Miner, Edna's brother-in-law, was concerned.

Edna said she lost control of the car, and after passing through a small ditch crunched a big Oak tree on Harold's side causing him to do a face plant in the windshield. The car had a driver-side air bag but none on the passenger side.

Harold stated that Edna lost control of the car while trying to punch him in the nose and once she realized that wouldn't work, because she couldn't drive and swing at the same time, intentionally ran into the tree, knowing she would be protected by the driver air bag. Harold wasn't seriously injured, other than a broken nose when he was thrown forward and cracked the windshield with his face. But, when he jumped out of the passenger window trying to avoid further pummeling from Edna, he slammed his head on a low hanging oak branch, poking out one eye and disabling the hearing capacity of his right ear.

When Sheriff Miner and the three-time State Association of Volunteer Firefighters "Best Organized Fundraiser" award-winning Hinkley County Volunteer Fire and Rescue arrived to dislodge Edna from the air bag that had tangled around her neck, they found Harold several yards from the car lying face down in some deer dung, unconscious but still breathing. They assumed he had been thrown from the car by the impact.

It was only later, after the sheriff's traffic report had already been filed, that Harold regained consciousness and revealed the real facts of the case. He wanted Edna charged with attempted murder, or at least attempting to cause serious injury through use of a motor vehicle without an airbag, if there was such a felonious act. But after having a stern talk with Sheriff Miner, he backed off and admitted he may have instigated the disagreement. Sheriff Miner advised him he better look for a car with dual air bags.

The couple reconciled after Sheriff Miner reminded Harold of Edna's half interest in the hardware store.

Harold squinted at the audience, trying to make a raw count with his one good eye. The effort made him feel like his fake eye, which always looked a little to the left making him appear cross-eyed, was going to pop out of the socket. Over one hundred people sat in the audience, all staring at him, waiting for the meeting to be called to order.

Harold once again moved closer to the microphone and repeated, "Uh, one, two, three." No feedback came and the amplified sound quieted the restless crowd.

"Well, we are happy you all found the time to come to our meetin' this evening. I think you will find it worth your time. We are fortunate to have a guest this evening that is on the cusp of an exciting new technology, that not only will save you money, but will save our good old planet as well. And as you know, it's the only one we got." Some heads nodded, agreeing at least about the planet thing.

"You all know, I ain't one to go gamble my money away at the Olatagwa Reservation Casino, so, it's the same thing when a deal comes along that seems to be too good to be true. I give it a long hard look before ever getting involved. But friends, this is one of those deals where you just can't lose. What's free'er than wind? It's like God himself is up there with his cheeks all puffed out blowing the money back in your pocket." The crowd rumbled as they whispered to each other and moved to the edge of their seats.

"Now, I guess I been ramblin' on long enough. Let's let the expert bring you up to speed on this here, well, this here project... I guess you could call it that. Sittin' next to me here is Ripple Wonaff, civil engineer, graduating suma cum laddie from the University of, of... Which one was it, Rip?"

Rip leaned toward Harold and cupped his hand away from the microphone. "I didn't say."

Harold, having his good ear turned away from Rip, misunderstood. "The University of *Disney*?" Harold smiled and said, "Surprised you didn't major in cartoons." The crowd erupted in spontaneous laughter as if on queue. "So, Rip, tell us about this modern marvel of engineering."

The Cast

Rip took his time scooting back from the table and standing. He dressed casual, knit shirt with chinos and loafers. One didn't want to overdress when dealing with a bunch of country folk. One needed to come down to their level, at least dress-wise, although he didn't own any coveralls. Pulling the microphone from the cradle, he swung the cord over Harold's head and moved to an open area of the stage, allowing for a few seconds of dramatic pause.

He drew his fingers through his hair, closed his eyes like he was in silent meditation or prayer for several seconds, and then drew the mic to his lips. The crowd noise dwindled in anticipation. Rip eyed the audience with intensity and then said with authority, "Wind, W-I-N-D, spells wind. Something man has studied, written about, philosophized about…Lied about…" He paused, raising his hand in an arcing motion. "The wind was so strong and blew so hard it turned the sheep's wool into a sweater while it was still on its back." A chuckle came from the crowd but concerned attention still prevailed. He had the crowd where he wanted them.

"How many of you hate to see that power-company bill come every month? Come on, hold up those hands." Rip threw his arm in the air. "That's right. Oh, I see one feller in the back with his arms crossed. Must work for the power company." Everyone strained to see who Rip was talking about. "Ain't nothing wrong with that." Rip turned and said, as if he were talking to himself, "You might want to consider another line of work though, after I finish here tonight.

"See folks," Rip pulled himself up onto the table and took a seat, getting casual and hiding Harold from the view of the audience, "we are entering a new era, an era of self sufficiency; freedom from the bonds of high utility bills. And do you know what gives us that freedom…? Wind. W-I-N-D. That's right, wind. That summer breeze…; that winter draft that comes under the door…; that up-draft that helps the eagle soar…; that frightening thunderstorm that makes the sky roar." Rip stood and started pacing across the stage, as he grew louder. "*That* my friends is *power*; un-leashed power that's just waiting to make your lives more comfortable. It'll undo the shackles of the power company that drains your checkbook every month. It'll put the power back in your hands." The crowd rose in raucous applause, holding their hands up clapping, whistling, and hooting.

Rip raised his hands signaling quiet and turned to Harold, who had moved next to Martha so he was exposed to the audience again, and commented loud enough for the microphone to pick up, "Harold, you have quite an intelligent group here. I'm impressed."

Harold nodded and smiled.

"Now folks," Rip continued, using hand gestures, squeezing his forehead, and shaking his head to emphasize his point, "I'm used to dealing with skeptics, people that can't think for themselves. You know the ones; they wait for the government to tell them what to do, hoping to get a handout. No, I can tell, it's easy for me to see, that ain't the case with this group."

A few more whistles and some clapping affirmed Rip's intuitive observation.

The Lure

Harold stood and moved next to Rip and took the microphone, almost as if the move were choreographed. "We appreciate you bein' so kindly and recognizing the quality of this community. We work to keep this town presentable and we don't allow no riff-raff, if you know what I mean. But Rip, you've got these people on the edge of their seats. Let's get to the meat of the subject. Tell them the good part; how they can get involved."

Rip took the microphone and leaned against the table again, getting relaxed. "I guess I have been rambling on a little. But, you know, I get so excited when I come to a new town like this and see the potential; see the raw courage of the town's people and their will to aspire to new heights. Well, it just sends shivers all the way down to my toes." Rip looked at his tasseled loafer, smiled, and said, "And they're darn nice toes."

That drew another chuckle.

Rip held up his hand and turned to Harold, who was whispering in Martha's ear with one cupped hand and fondling her back with the other, and said, "Mr. Hanover, uh, pardon the interruption, but could you get the model we looked at before the program started?"

Martha, her face blushed, resumed looking down at her steno pad and taking notes and Harold, buttoning his suit coat before standing, abruptly left the stage to retrieve the prop.

Harold returned and pushed the rolling square table toward the middle of the stage. A large cloth covered it with a tent like spire in the center.

"Now, you all have to use a little imagination here, but think what it would be like to never pay a power bill again." Rip gingerly pulled the cloth away from the table, revealing a miniature farm setting; house, barn, garage, and small shed spread out with a white picket fence surrounding. Set in the middle of the picturesque model was a white spire with a propeller on top.

Rip looked off-stage at Harold, who was standing next to the wall supporting the bank of light switches and nodded. Rip reached under the table and pulled out a small electric fan as the lights began to dim. He started the fan that turned the propeller, and at the same time pushed the button on the battery pack hanging under the table.

Lights came on in every model building as well as a miniature yard light. The audience strained to see the model, emitting oohs and ahs as they watched the propeller spin.

"And it's all free as the wind," Rip said, smiling and holding the fan.

"But what if the wind don't blow?" The question came from some darkened part of the hall.

"That's a darn good question. See, Harold. I told you, these people are thinkers." Rip tripped the button on the fan and the propeller slowly stopped spinning, but the lights on the model stayed on. "What happens when the wind don't blow…? Nothing happens. What happens when the wind don't blow at your house now? The power company don't stop sending you power. So when the winds don't blow, you just go back to the expensive power company and use their expensive electricity for maybe a day. 'Cause you and I both know, the wind may stop blowin', but it don't stop for long, and when it starts blowin' again, the old turbine starts turnin', and the free electricity starts flowin'. And that, my friends, is a simple as it gets."

The Hook

Harold flipped the house lights on and walked back on the stage as Rip covered the model and pushed it to the back of the stage.

Harold put his arm around Rip and said, squinting at the audience through his one good eye and smiling, "That's quite a demonstration, Rip. Now, here's the important question. How do these good folks get on board with this, this, whatever you want to call it; this project? I mean, the power company sure ain't gonna come out to their house and put up somethin' that's gonna put 'em out of business. Now that's a fact."

Rip shrugged to loosen Harold's hug and stepped away. "I'll be honest with you folks, these turbines aren't cheap. Even though I have a direct connection with the manufacturer, they are still a pretty penny to get built and get installed. But once it's there, it ain't going anywhere and all it will ever do is make you money. And just think, if you ever wanted to sell out, say retire and move to that condo in Florida, what do you think that potential buyer's gonna think when you say, *power bill*, what power bill?

"Now, here are some facts to consider. For those of you who decide tonight, saying to yourself, this might be something I want to get on board with, take the next step so to speak, there are some extra benefits. First, the government finally did something smart. They are willing to give you back $1500 of the cost of this moneymaker, no strings attached other than you only have until the end of this year to get the project completed. Second, for those of you who were smart enough to come tonight and be enlightened, I'm going to take another twenty percent off the final cost. Take that into consideration along with the money you will save over the next five years on your power bill and you might say the whole thing is free. That's right, free. And there ain't nothing better than free."

A man near the back stood, thumbs entwined in his dirty bib coverall straps, and said, "How much do one of these contraptions cost?"

Rip strained to see who asked the question. "And your name sir, if I may ask?"

He hesitated, whispered to his wife and then stood again. "It's Letterman. Roger Letterman. I guess it don't matter, you all know me anyway."

"Well, Roger, the cost varies depending on the size and height of the unit. But, we are probably talking around ten thousand dollars."

A rumble of cautious whispering came from the crowd.

"But let me ask you a question, Roger. How much did you pay for your last tractor?"

Roger chuckled and looked at his wife with a smirk. "Ain't bought a tractor for twenty years and the last one was used."

"I can understand that. But I bet it cost more than ten thousand dollars and I also bet, other than being a good tractor, it never lowered your power bill."

The crowd murmured their approval as Roger sat back down and crossed his beefy arms with some attitude, like a child who had been ridiculed by a teacher.

Rip continued, "I'll tell you what, Roger, come on up here to the stage. You look like a man that knows how to deal. Come on, don't be shy. Bring the little woman with you." The wife was anything but little. She no doubt tipped the scales at over two hundred and had a tough time finding stretch pants, even in the plus sizes.

The two consulted and Roger, the carved frown lines in his face piling up like stacked wood, shook his bald head, turning down the invitation.

Rip smiled and said, "I know, no one wants to be the first in line, but believe me, it'll be worth your while. Come on now, how about it, folks, let's give a big round of applause for the Lettermans, and see if we can persuade 'em to come on up here."

The crowd responded, urging Roger to go to the stage. Someone sitting behind him put his boot up against Roger's chair and gave it a shove, pushing Roger out of the seat and causing him to inadvertently stand up. The crowd erupted in applause. Now he had no choice, relented, and grabbed his wife by the sleeve of her sweater and they meandered up to the stage.

Rip welcomed them as they climbed to the stage and held his hands up, quieting the crowd. He shook both of their hands, getting names during the introduction and then put his arm around Wanda, at least as much of her as he could. While everyone had been watching Roger and Wanda approach the stage, Rip had asked Harold for a little background on the Lettermans.

"Okay Roger, on that farm of yours, how may acres is it?"

Roger surveyed the audience and then looked at Wanda and she nodded. "'Bout a hundred, give or take a fence row."

"Sounds nice. And how many hogs do you have at one time in that farrowing house?"

"Anywhere's from fifty to a hunert," Roger said, scratching the stubble on his chin.

"And how much does it cost to heat that barn in the winter?" Rip smiled at the audience.

Roger turned to Wanda. "Whataya think?"

Wanda pulled at her stretch pants, pondering the question. "Two or three hundred a month, I suspect. Don't have to keep it too warm. Pigs don't mind."

"Okay, that's fair." Rip acted as though he was punching a calculator in his hands and said, "That's about thirty-six hundred a year, and that's just for the farrowing house. But let's make this fair; after all, the power company execs didn't drive their Mercedes and Cadillacs down here tonight to answer questions. So, let's say your power bill runs about four thousand dollars a year. I know you all in the audience already did the math. Like I said, we got some thinkers in this room. Since you don't have that power bill to pay, that ten thousand dollar investment paid for itself in three years with money left over to make a down payment on that new tractor."

Roger was still staring off into the distance doing the math in his head, but his wife was looking over her shoulder at the model that sat near the edge of the stage. She turned to Rip and asked, "It'll heat the house too, huh?"

Rip smiled at her and winked. He stood between the couple and put his arms around them and began, "Enough sales talk, let's get down to business. Wanda, you seem to be the financier in this family, so, what if I said for just a five hundred dollar down-payment, you can be first in line to have a Genteric G-200 wind-power turbine installed at your farm. Are you ready to pull the trigger? Be the first farm in Hinkley County to never pay a power bill again?"

Roger spoke up first with alarm. "Five hunert *dollars*?"

Rip countered his apparent displeasure by saying, "That's almost as much as Wanda pays every month to the power company. Isn't that right, Wanda?"

Wanda shrugged and said, "When we gotta pay the rest?"

"We set you up on a nice payment plan that I guarantee will be less than what you would have paid the power company every month for as long as you can remember. You write me the check tonight and I'll come to the ranch and we'll lay out the plan and sign the contracts tomorrow."

A few comments came from the crowd like, "Come on Roger, what you waitin' for?" and "Go on, Roger, you sell a couple more bottles of moonshine and you'll never miss it."

Rip made a last pitch. "Wanda, you might be surprised what happens if you write that check."

Wanda looked at Roger and he just shrugged again. Wanda opened her purse that she had been clutching. "We don't write no checks." She searched around in the tattered purse and without pulling her hand out and showing any of the contents, she counted out five one hundred dollar bills.

Rip smiled. "Looky here, folks. The Lettermans just made history. They are the first farm in Hinkley County to step into the future. These are brave people, willing to take a chance, just like the pioneers that homesteaded here and took a chance that this county would turn into the fine community we see today. Well, Roger and Wanda, I'm going to reward you for being brave enough to step forward when the rest of your neighbors have second thoughts. Here, Wanda, put that hard earned money back in your purse. I'm not taking your money tonight. Your down payment is paid in full. Martha, make a note of that."

Roger and Wanda looked at each other and smiled.

"Who's gonna be next? Who wants to be the second most luckiest person in Hinkley County?"

A tall man dressed in a black suit ambled up to the stage, his backward collar, shining gold chain and cross, exposed for Rip to see.

"Ah, a man of the cloth," Rip said, smiling.

"I have listened to your presentation, Mr. Ripple, and I believe our ministry could benefit from your project. I would like to sign up and be the first commercial establishment in town to utilize God's free wind. I think it's only appropriate that it be God's house that reaps the benefit." He presented a forceful appearance for a man dedicated to such a peaceful endeavor. His six feet of ministerial presence was accentuated by his black suit and coarse black mane pulled back in a '50s ducktail, making him resemble Johnny Cash without the guitar strapped to his chest.

Rip took in the mystical aura of the man and then smiled. He had once again been blessed with an opportunity. "Reverend, I could not have said it better myself. And of what religious persuasion are you?"

The reverend stiffened, raising one eyebrow and gave Rip a threatening stare, acting as if he were offended by the question before eyeing the crowd and seeing only familiar faces. He then relented, answering the question with part distain and yet a tone of appreciation for the opportunity to announce his affiliation with the Lord. "Why, I'm Baptist, son, wouldn't have it any other way."

"Was saved myself through Baptism, total emersion by the way, and have never looked back, Reverend. My whole life changed the day I took the dunk. It will be an honor and a privilege to work with you and your church." Rip stepped away and spoke to the crowd that continued to gather around the stage. "This is what I'm talking about, folks. Your own head of the Baptist church is stepping up and trusting in God to bless his flock with free electricity. It doesn't get any better than that. The good reverend is going to step right over to Martha and make his deposit and she will give him his receipt."

The pastor pulled a check from his suit coat pocket and waved it above his head for all to see.

Rip put his arm around the reverend and leaned in like they were posing for a picture and daintily plucked the check from his fingers. "And let me show you what I am going to do with this check." Rip took a step closer to the gawking crowd and raising the check, tore it into pieces and tossed it into the air. "Do you notice a pattern here, folks? Who wants to be the next in line?"

Another burly man in coveralls pushed his way through the group gathered around Rip, pulling his checkbook out and looking at Harold Hanover. "Harold, what say you about this? You signed up?"

Harold, who had slipped his foot out of his loafer and was sliding his toe up and down Martha's leg under the table looked up and smiled. "You bet'cha. I know'd this was a good thing as soon as I met ol' Rip here. If you saw my power bill, you'd understand why I was first to sign the papers. Why, that sign in front of my store alone needs its own power plant."

The big man looked down at his checkbook as he pulled on one ear and contemplated, then said, "Where do I sign?"

Rip looked at the check the man was holding, searching for a name, and said, "George, you own a farm?"

"Dairy, milk two hundred and fifty Jerseys every mornin' and every evenin'."

"My grandpappy had cows," Rip said, scratching his chin. "Damn hard work and had to scrape to make a living." Rip reached down and took the check. "I'm sure you have it tough too." Rip held up the check and tore it into pieces. "Now you go over there and give Martha your information so we can get that generator pumpin' money into your pocket."

The Catch

The crowd pushed closer to the stage in a growing frenzy as more of the check pieces littered the floor. Hands held up cash and others scrambled to write checks, waving them in the air trying to draw Rip's attention.

Rip started to reach for another customer's check but stopped and pulled his cell phone from his pocket. "Just a minute, folks, I've got to take this call. You all just give Martha your personal information and the money and when I'm done here I'll continue to talk to each one of you."

The attention turned to Martha as she scrambled to collect the cash and checks and write names and addresses.

Rip stepped back into the shadows of the stage curtain, feigning conversation on his cell phone. So far, he could not have asked for better results. His only concern was a tall, dark complexioned cowboy who had lurked in the shadows all evening, never responding like the rest of the crowd and now leaving while everyone else gathered around the stage. He didn't look like a cop, but in these small towns, you could never tell. He made a mental note to watch for a tail when he left the school.

Rip returned, but only after he was sure most of the audience had signed. An additional forty names were added to the list, which was still growing. Everyone waited in anticipation of Rip's next gesture of kindness, assuming the trend of benevolence would continue and their check would be the next one destroyed or their cash would be returned. Instead, Rip stood back and watched as the last hundred-dollar bill was collected, and the last name was added to the list.

Harold bundled the currency and checks and placed them in a bank pouch.

Rip held up his hands and immediately had everyone's attention. "Folks, thanks for coming tonight. It's been my pleasure and you will hear from me soon, so we can get the electricity flowin' and those power bills stoppin'." Rip turned and snatched the money pouch from Harold and headed for the rear door of the auditorium.

Several people yelled at his back, "Hey, what about me?" And, "Do I get my money back?"

That was the last time anyone in Hinkley County ever saw Ripple Wonaff.

Chapter 2

By the time it became apparent no one was going to hear from Ripple Wonaff, the checks he had collected were cashed and the dream of free electricity turned into a nightmarish realization of being hustled by a carnival huckster.

Harold Hanover hovered over his bowl of Cheerios while Edna moved around the kitchen, unnecessarily cleaning with a dishtowel while she verbally admonished him.

"I just can't believe that after thirty years in retail, you still can't recognize a scam, even when it slaps you in the face. I told you the first time you mentioned this, this wind thing, that it sounded fishy to me. What did I tell you? Find out who he is. Find out where he's from. Find out…just find out. But, *oh no*, you couldn't take my advice. No, you had to jump in with both feet; make that stupid model along with giving him a check for a thousand dollars that we will never see again."

"Reg said he was—"

"I don't *care* what my brother-in-law said. You think a small-town sheriff is going to be able to find that crook? And even if he does, you think that's going to get our money back? And then after the meeting, you go spend half the night with him. What did you do, help him count the money? You probably paid for his dinner. I just don't know, Harold. I just don't know."

The brow beating had started the day after the meeting and hadn't stopped since. His only sanctuary was the hardware store, at least when Edna wasn't there, so he hurried to finish his breakfast. "I've got to get to the store. There's a salesman coming in from Chicago." He knew as soon as he made up the excuse for leaving early, that it was a mistake.

"What's this one going to sell you, invisible ink? Or maybe shovels that dig holes on their own? How about chickens that lay golden eggs, we could use one of those."

"It's just the Jergans Hardware man. I've got to order screws." Harold pushed the empty bowl toward the middle of the table and hurried to make his exit before Edna began another session of verbal abuse.

◆　◆　◆

Business at the hardware had taken an abrupt downward turn since the disappearance of Ripple Wonaff, and Harold's unintentional participation in the scam. The Chamber of Commerce board of directors had even held a special meeting to discuss Harold's possible impeachment, but after thorough research of the organization's bylaws, they discovered no reference to the methodology of impeachment of an elected president. Therefore, they decided not to hold any more meetings until his term ended and a new leader could be selected.

Harold sat at his desk behind the main cashier counter and paged through a catalogue of string trimmers without actually looking at the pictures. He was daydreaming about his evening spent with Martha Redman at the Cougar Falls Best Western after the meeting in the high school auditorium. Every once in a while, a tinge of remorse would invade his thoughts; not one of the sanctity of his marriage, but rather the thought that if he had kept close to Rip, as Edna supposed he had, the scoundrel may not have had the opportunity to skip town.

The bell above the front door of the store tinkled and Red Redderson, editor of the twice-weekly *Hinkley Messenger*, stepped in. The wrinkled suit he had on along with the stained tie enhanced his short stature. His vision of the desk was obscured by the cash register and he yelled, "Harold, you in here?"

Harold sighed, closed the catalogue, and rose from the swivel chair that emitted a loud squeak. Redderson had already written and published a lengthy article about the great Hinkley windmill scam, as it was now known, in his prior issue and Harold was not interested in participating in a follow-up story. Thankfully, he was a pretty steady advertiser in the *Messenger* and Red had left his name out.

"Something I can help you with, Red? I've got a new line of string trimmers, guaranteed to start or your money back, no questions asked."

Redderson leaned against the counter, sweat bleeding through the armpit of his suit. "Naw, the trailer park takes care of all that. Thought you might be interested though, I just came from the sheriff's office and Marge says when they finally figured up all the people that got scammed, it came to over twenty thousand dollars. I heard he got you for over a grand. That right?"

Harold's stomach rolled and his Cheerios pushed back up his throat. "The sheriff say anything about finding the rascal? That's what's important. I'd say his days as sheriff are numbered if he doesn't come up with something pretty soon."

"Pretty tough talk considering he's your brother-in-law." Redderson pawed through a candy dish Harold had on the counter. "How did you get mixed up with Wonaff anyway? He just wanders in here off the street?"

Harold didn't trust Redderson. "I don't think I got mixed up with anything. He was a legitimate inquiry to the Chamber of Commerce and ended up talking to me."

"Really." Redderson's sideways accusatory stare caused his bloodshot eyes to bulge. "And nobody at the Chamber did any checking into his background or anything? With the Internet these days, it's not that hard. Took me about thirty seconds. I found a bio written by a parole officer in California."

Harold's Cheerios flopped again.

"You know how he got that unusual name, Ripple?"

Harold just shrugged, knowing he was going to get the information whether he wanted to know or not.

"His daddy was an alchy, and his favorite way to start the day was to drink a bottle of Ripple wine. It's this cheap wine that —"

"I know, I know," Harold said.

"Anyway, I suppose he had just finished his first bottle when he and the old lady were deciding on a name. Anyway, his rap sheet, just in California, is as long as your arm, mostly small-time stuff, forgery, passing bad paper, credit-card fraud, stuff like that. Funny, he used his real name. Usually, a guy like that will have twenty aliases, but he seems to think he's above the law, or at least two or three steps ahead of 'em."

Redderson turned, resting his back against the counter and looked out the front window of the store. "Yeah, I bet he's living high right now. Twenty-plus big ones in one score, and what, he got you for three or four thousand, at least that's what I heard."

"It was only a thousand."

Redderson turned and smiled. Harold slumped back down in his chair.

Redderson said, "They'll catch up with him eventually. Trouble is, the money will all be spent and whatever court gets the case will figure what's the use of wasting taxpayer money putting him in jail. They'll put him on probation again and slap his hands. Yeah, it's a shame, a crying shame."

Harold prayed for another customer to come in the store. He pulled a roll of Tums out of his desk drawer and chewed three.

"Stomach a little foamy, Harold? Understandable, given what's happened. How's business? I could get you a full-page insert; sell a few of those string trimmers. I mean, I was going to run this follow-up story on the wind thing, you know, who lost what, that kind of stuff. I mean, you took the biggest hit, so I would have to include that."

There it was. Laid out like a stretch of newly paved highway. Buy a big, unnecessary ad in my paper or I'll run a big story about how you helped the entire town get swindled by a carnival huckster.

Redderson stayed silent, letting the insinuation linger in the air like sour cigar smoke while he pawed through the candy dish again, occasionally glancing up at Harold who was rubbing his forehead.

Might as well just throw the cards on the table and make his call. "So, if I'm getting the *point* here," Harold said, "if I buy some big ad or insert in your rag paper, you'll forego any follow-up story on the wind thing. That right?"

"*Harold*," Redderson said, "I could get offended. I mean, I would never let ad dollars sway my journalistic duty to deliver the news in a fair, compassionate, and just manner. The people of this fine community expect me to investigate and —"

"Cut the crap, Red. We both know that's what you meant. To be honest with you, I can't afford any advertising right now. So run your story. Business can't get any worse."

Redderson, being the true champion of the journalistic credo, never let an insult get in the way of a good story, put the ad-extortion plan on the back burner and moved on. "So, this global warming thing, you think it's for real? I mean, you bit on the wind-turbine thing pretty hard."

Harold sighed. "Look Red, I've got a meeting with my accountant this afternoon and I've got stuff I have to get ready."

"Martha Redman your accountant?" Redderson had been staring at the candy dish and slowly looked up with a wry smile. "Don't forget to sharpen your pencil before the meeting."

The bell above the door tinkled and both men turned to see Ray Chicken Hawk Lightfeather walk through the door. Ray was one of the few remaining Olatagwa Indian blood descendents still living in Hinkley County, and he carried the moniker with pride. His black hair was long and braided under a full-brimmed Stetson trimmed out with a long chicken hawk tail feather in the band. In his mid-sixties, Ray still had meaningful stature, carrying his cowboy-boot-enhanced six-foot plus height with dignified elegance. His leather vest boasted elk-antler buttons and his belt buckle, studded with turquoise and tanzanite, would make Elizabeth Taylor blush with envy.

Ray left Hinkley when he was young, after dropping out of high school, and hitch hiked to California, hoping to use his rough dark complexion, high cheek bones, and hook nose to secure secondary parts in the many western movies popular in the early '60s. Over the years, his resume of bit parts grew to include being killed in over twenty B movies without ever speaking a line of dialogue.

The highlight of his career came when he was selected to have a subordinate starring role in an episode of *Little House On The Prairie*. The drama called for Ray to be an Indian who had been lost on the prairie and lying by the side of the wagon path for some unknown reason, found by Charles Ingalls, Michael Landon's character, and brought back to the little house to be saved from his apparent lack of Indian survival skills. All Ray had to do was grunt once in a while and play sick while the plot thickened around him with all of the regular characters and town's people playing their regular roles and bringing tense drama to the weekly series.

Sometime during the filming, which was done on a sound stage at a beautiful ranch in Simi Valley, California, far from the harsh prairie, on a day when Ray wasn't part of the production and didn't have to lay in the loft and occasionally grunt, he went into town and proceeded to get outrageously drunk. He then returned to the ranch in his decked-out four-wheeler and did donuts around the fake Ingalls' house and barn, eventually rolled the truck in the fake corral, breaking his collarbone and one arm.

Ray spent the next ten days in the Simi Valley jail on a bunk, much the same as the one in the loft that was used on the sound stage, feeling sick and occasionally grunting.

The director re-shot the scenes Ray had been in with another less-authentic Indian look alike, and sent Ray a bill for the lost production time, just shy of eighty-seven thousand dollars.

Ray left Hollywood and returned to Hinkley County, where he was revered for his acting prowess and star-studded accomplishments for a few months and then settled into the routine of being a normal unemployed resident.

He opened a car lot with a cowboy and Indian theme, but got sued by Fred Ribley of Fred's Fords after he ran a commercial on the local country-radio station claiming he could get special government financing and discounts through the Bureau of Indian Affairs for anyone with or without Indian ancestry. The lawsuit, along with an investigation by the State Attorney General's office alleging odometer tampering and title fraud, led to the demise of the car lot.

Ray sold water wands to local farmers for a while, claiming an Osage Indian Shaman blessed them and they could pinpoint water sources up to a mile deep.

He sold a mysterious oily substance he said came from a centuries-old Indian formula that when applied to cow udders would double milk production. Sales plummeted after a local dairy farmer had the liquid analyzed by the state dairy cooperative chemist and he reported the substance to be used motor oil laced with peppermint extract.

Fortunately for Ray, when finally he was too broke to afford a new pair of boots, the Olatagwa Indian Tribe Counsel, which now had offices in the Willis Tower in downtown Chicago, decided to open a casino on land they claimed had been illegally confiscated by the state park system not far from Hinkley. Profits would be partially divided among Olatagwa descendents by virtue of proven ancestry. This was an easy accomplishment for Ray since his mother was pure-bred Olatagwa and his father had skipped before his birth and remained unknown.

After years of legal battles over right of ownership of a portion of the Olatagwa State Park, the casino was built and operational and Ray received one-tenth of one-percent of the profit portion set aside for Olatagwa descendents. The check arrived the first of each month and Ray once again became a prominent resident of Hinkley County.

Harold and Ray were about the same age but had grown up in different worlds. Harold's family took a prominent roll in the small town as storeowner. Ray was an Indian without a father and the social barriers were high and strong. Over the years, Harold got to know Ray but kept his distance, still mired in the racial undertone of his youth.

Ray Chicken Hawk Lightfeather spoke very softly with an almost feminine inflection that led Harold to suspect that he had acquired some unusual sexual habits while masquerading as an actor in Hollywood. No one had ever seen Ray with a female companion, but on the other hand, no one had ever seen him with a male companion either, so the rumors Harold had heard remained just that, rumors. Given Ray's size and ominous presence, there were no volunteers to confront him about the issue.

Ray walked through the store as if stalking retail prey, never making eye contact with Harold or Red.

Harold saw the opportunity to distance himself from Redderson's extortion ploy and addressed Ray as he stopped in front of the chain saw display. Harold yelled across the room, "Ray, how we doing today. That McCullough will chew through a cord of wood an hour. You heat your teepee with wood?"

Ray slowly turned, his deep-set black dots for eyes delivering a penetrating lack of response to Harold's racial slur.

Harold heard the tinkle of the doorbell as Red hurried out and up the street. The quick retreat was not unexpected. Red had a genuine fear of Ray Lightfeather due to an unfortunate disagreement about a story he had written on the Hinkley *Messenger's* editorial page about the Olatagwa casino. Red had taken a stand against the casino prior to its construction, and editorialized that it would lead to an influx of unsavory characters, prostitution, chronic gambling disease, and a host of other problems the community didn't need or want.

Ray had taken exception to the editorial and came to the *Messenger's* office the day following the printing of the story carrying a tomahawk and dressed in hand-sewn leather pants, a vest with fringe, moccasins, and war paint on his face and stood in the lobby for one entire day without comment, merely intimidating any customer who entered.

Ray broke his stare to look at the door as Red departed and then turned back to Harold as he walked up the aisle. Ray rested an arm on a shelf, getting comfortable.

Harold gulped, trying to push his Cheerios back down his throat. "Bad joke, about the teepee, sorry. Uh, anything I can do for you today, Ray?"

Ray's black pupils emphasized his dark skin and deep-set eyes. When he spoke, it was a lilting high pitch, which had a startling effect coming from such a big man even though Harold had heard it many times before. Ray asked, "This wind thing, you still involved?"

Harold reached in his pocket for some more Tums, legs trembling. "Look, I'm sorry if you got taken by that guy. *Really*," Harold pleaded, "I had no idea. I mean, I lost a bunch too." Harold envisioned Ray pulling out one of those big Bowie knives and engraving Indian hieroglyphics on his chest.

"What you mean, got taken?" Sometimes Ray reverted back to playing Tonto and speaking broken English, just to give credibility to his Indian heritage and, some thought, hide his lack of intelligent vocabulary.

"Well, you know, the guy skipped town… Wait, I don't remember seeing your name on the list. Were you at the schoolhouse?" Harold sensed that Ray's intimidating stare might be one of stupidity rather than animosity so he tried to change the flow of the conversation. "What's your interest, I mean, are you looking for the guy or something?"

Ray relaxed a little more and took his hat off, brushed at an imaginary smudge before slowly looking up and reestablishing his intimidating stare. "You mean your friend that stole all the money?"

Harold's stomach started gurgling like a plugged up sink and he was feeling feint. He glanced at the store's front window, searching for witnesses on the street but saw none. He gulped and said, "Okay, let's start over. You are interested in something to do with the wind, we talking electricity here?"

Ray put his hat back on like he was glad they were finally getting to the point. "Heard you have deal to sell windmills. Something Chicken Hawk may be interested in." Ray also liked to talk about himself in the third person.

Taking Ray's lead Harold responded, "Is Chicken Hawk interested in buying a wind turbine, for Chicken Hawk's tee...uh ...home?"

"Where you get these things, these tur – bines? They cost a lot?" Ray pulled a leather pouch out of his vest, unzipped it, and fished around until he found an acceptable chunk of what appeared to be dried meat. He ripped a chunk off with his teeth and chewed. He held his hand out, offering Harold what remained of the piece of jerky.

Harold hesitated, evaluating the significance of the offer. Certain Indian social nuances were attributable to offering of food or gift, and he didn't want to offend the Chicken Hawk. But the thought of ingesting a chunk of half-eaten spoiled meat was about to make him puke. "Uh, just finished breakfast, so, no thanks."

Ray chewed. "What they cost?"

"The turbines? Well, I've heard as much as ten thousand dollars for a small one and a lot more for those big ones like you see on TV. You ... Is Chicken Hawk thinking about buying one?"

Ray popped the last chunk of jerky into his mouth, chewed a few times, and then worked with his fingernail to dislodge some of the stringy meat from a rear molar. "Casino. Casino interested. My uncle run the maintenance department. Chicken Hawk talk to him about buying tur – bines. Maybe you and Chicken Hawk do business, huh?"

"Look Ray...Chicken Hawk... I don't know that much about these things. The casino has to use giga watts of electricity. I don't know if these things are designed for that kind of consumption. You know what I mean?"

"You find out how much they cost and call Chicken Hawk." Ray handed Harold a business card. The card had a flying chicken hawk in the corner and the name *Lightfeather Investments* emblazoned in gold with a single phone number underneath.

Ray raised his hand, palm out in traditional Indian salutation and walked toward the door.

"But, but, what if I can't, don't…Ray?" But it was too late as the bell tinkled and Ray turned to walk down the street.

CHAPTER 3

Nub sat at the dinner table, one elbow and hand supporting his chin and the other hand pushing some peas around his plate with a fork, attempting to get them in a straight line. His real name, Nubert, after his paternal grandfather, had eventually been shortened to Nub because he was born several weeks premature and never quite grew into himself. Nub's parents, Roger and Wanda Letterman sat at opposite ends of the table, emptied dinner plates in front of them awaiting removal, looking at their latest power bill from the Tri-County Electric Cooperative.

Nub, still staring at the peas said, "Can I go now? I got stuff I need to do."

"Should'a know'd he was a con man by the way he smiled all the time," Wanda said. "You notice that? And he had those shifty eyes. You looked at him and you knew he was about to pick your pocket."

Roger stared at the power bill. "Sounded good though. You see all that garbage on the TV and you can't help but think it's true. We was lucky to be the first in line though. Oh, well." Roger tossed the bill on the pile of other un-opened envelopes in the middle of the table.

"I have things I need to *do*," Nub repeated.

Wanda flicked a dead fly off the table and then scratched her chin. "Nub, you know dinner is the only time we get to see you. It ain't gonna hurt you to sit for a while."

Roger leaned back and rested his folded hands on his overall bib. "I suppose you're in a hurry to get on that damned computer thing again. Ever since you figured out how to wire that gizmo antenna out on the barn, you spend all your time slurpin' the web, or whatever you call it. I call it a waste of time. I can't get a lick'a work out'a you anymore. Mom, you're gonna have to talk to him now, I'm not kiddin'."

Wanda looked up and frowned. "Why me? You're his father. You should be the one to lay down the law."

Nub moved his gaze from one parent to the other as they conversed about him, like he was watching a ping-pong match.

"Oh yeah, well who insisted he couldn't get along in life without a damned computer? Oh Roger, he needs one so he can keep up with the other kids at school," Roger mimicked Wanda. "He's the smartest kid in the school now, why's he need somethin' to make him smarter? I wish I knew where he got all the brains so's I could go buy some. It sure weren't from your side of the family."

"Oh, go slop your hogs and quit complainin'."

Nub rose from the table and started rifling through drawers.

"What you lookin' for?" Wanda asked, scooting back in anticipation of helping with the search.

"I had a USB cable that I brought home from the school lab in a baggy along with a zip drive. It had all my notes from the lab on it. It was on the table last night and was gone this morning, anyone seen it?"

Roger and Wanda looked at each other with lost expressions.

Roger responded, "I ain't seen any baggies on the table today. Maybe it's in your backpack. By the way, did you get those feed bags down from the loft like I asked?"

Nub continued his search.

Wanda tried to be stern. "Nub, your daddy asked you a question."

"Do you know that every second there are over a trillion bits of information dispersed on the Internet?" Nub didn't look up. "So, while I'm searching for my zip drive that someone probably threw away because they didn't know what it was, I'm missing, what, several hundred trillion bits of information. Did you ever consider that?"

Roger threw his hands up and stomped out of the kitchen, allowing the screen door slam to voice his anger.

Wanda scooted her chair back as silently as she could and took a look in the wastebasket that sat next to the kitchen counter. She pushed the top layer of discards aside and saw a zip lock baggy. She glanced at Nub, who continued to rummage through another drawer, and when she thought the time was right, reached down and snagged the baggie and scooted back up to the table.

A minute later, his mother said, "Oh, look here, is this what you are looking for? It was under the table. Must have fallen off when we cleared it for dinner."

Nub turned and spied the baggie and smiled. "Thanks, Mom."

As Nub reached for the baggie she pulled it away. "Sit down, Nub. It ain't gonna hurt to miss a few more cabillion bites of whatever."

Nub reluctantly pulled out a chair and slumped down with his elbows on the table.

"Now, Nub, I know how much you like doin' that computer stuff but your daddy's got a lot to handle around here and could use some help. He don't ask you for much, but when he does, it would sure be nice if you would do as he asks." Wanda gave him a motherly smile. Nub returned the gesture. Both continued to look at one another.

"Well?" Wanda asked.

"Well, what?"

Wanda's smile disappeared. "Well, are you going to do what I ask? Are you going to help out around here?"

"When's the guy coming to lay out the plan for the wind turbine? I've been running a program that estimates the greatest wind current based on the topography of our land and the obstructions. I think I have the perfect spot."

Wanda sighed. "He ain't comin'. Like we was talkin' about. He skipped town with most everyone's money. Lucky for us, we didn't lose nothin' ceptin' our pride."

"So, there's not going to be any wind turbine?" Nub said with a hint of joy.

"Naw, it was all a scam. Should'a knowed, there ain't nothin' free in this life. Just remember that, Nub."

Nub jumped up and headed for the door.

"Where you going now? You going to get those feed sacks for your dad?"

Nub was out the door and headed for his personal sanctuary, a walled-off section of the barn that had once been the milk house. At Nub's urging, Roger had paneled and insulated the room, wired it with Nub's help, and from that point forward, he rarely had access to the locked door.

Nub was small for his age of twelve, didn't care much for the hygienic routine of washing, combing, or for that matter, cutting hair. His hair, being naturally curly, ended up as a big wad of unkempt Brillo pad on top of his head. He had a tendency to fancy a single

27

t-shirt, usually one with an advertisement he had scored for free, and wear it continuously until it ended up on the rag pile. When his mother insisted on washing, Nub would stand guard next the machine, bare chest, with his arms crossed until the cycle was completed, waiting to retrieve his treasure.

Nub was branded as gifted by the school guidance counselor after suffering through an extensive battery of tests used to determine IQ. The school nurse said Nub leaned toward autistic characteristics and should have special handling both at school and at home. Fortunately for Nub, no one else at the school paid any attention to the recommendations, so he was just considered odd.

The one thing everyone at the school recognized was that Nub was blessed with a special dose of intelligence. They had to just rely on their own judgment and assumption that a twelve year old who could breeze through college level calculus equations and calculate in his head the circumference of obtuse angled spheres, must be pretty freeking smart, and if he wanted to wear the same shirt and pair of shorts everyday, good for him.

Nub unlocked the door to his laboratory, as he called it, in the old milk house, and promptly booted up his computer and inserted the zip drive he had retrieved from the kitchen. At school, he had gone to the computer lab and installed a program he had written to access the program codes the school used to maintain their satellite internet access. Each month the provider changed the access code to prevent illegitimate access. So each month, Nub had to hack the system, get the code to keep his own access working since his mom and dad would never consider buying the service. When the dish antenna arrived via UPS, Nub told his parents the Internet was free to anyone who could afford an antenna.

Booting up the computer was like opening a gate that accessed the superhighway to the world. After Nub had read every book he could find in the Hinkley library about programming and computer code, his new knowledge was like having the key to the vault inside the gate to the world. Nub spent hours worming his way through the Internet, looking for opportunities to access hidden doorways, without felonious intent, but rather with adventurous fervor. He corresponded with hundreds of scientists about theory and hypothesis, infuriating many with his contentious attitude and what they called childish manner, not realizing they corresponded with a child. He spent hours researching subjects that intrigued and aroused his curiosity, and, until he had been introduced to the resources of the Internet, had been unfulfilled and unanswered.

His mother's explanation that the wind turbine was a bust came as good news because it created a challenge. Now Nub could complete his research and build his own wind turbine to support the energy use on the farm. So far he had only developed a plan for positioning the tower, but now he would have the task of developing a complete construction metric utilizing the basic ingredients of items he could salvage from the farm, find via the internet, or locate on his own at Hank's Army Surplus in Hinkley.

CHAPTER 4

Lou Little Hair Luchini sat behind a giant mahogany desk, his index finger wrapped around a large unlit Cuban cigar. He stared down at a printout of gambling receipts broken down by revenue districts within the casino. His dark Sicilian complexion was emphasized by his shiny, dark, thin hair combed straight back on his balding head. His triple chin bulged and then retracted as he moved his head up and down scanning the figures.

Joe Little Cloud Rondelo, chief financial officer of the casino, fidgeted in a plush leather chair in front of the desk. Rondelo, formerly known as Joe No-neck before joining the tribe and being re-named Little Cloud, was short and due to what everyone supposed was a birth defect (or perhaps he had been dropped on his head one too many times at an early age) had no neck. His head sat precariously between his shoulders like a cabbage between the outer leaves. He permed and bleached his hair with tight, short curls and always wore open-necked shirts because there was no place to fit a collar under his chin.

Lou looked up at Rondelo and frowned. "Dease numbers on the slots, they suck. You change the flop? Same thing on the blackjack, down ten percent. What gives?" Lou stuck an unlit cigar in his mouth and chewed as he looked back down at the spreadsheet.

"I dunno, boss. It's the recession, I guess. And it's the end of the month. It'll pick up as soon as the government checks go out. Nobody changed nothin'."

Lou continued to chew his cigar and analyze the numbers. Lou digested the raw tobacco as he chewed without spitting or in any obvious way, discarding the emulsified remains of the cigar. It would slowly disappear much like a smoked cigar, only from the other end.

The Olatagwa Indian Reservation Management Company, LLC was located on the fifty-eighth floor of the Willis Tower in Chicago. Their suite of offices looked out over Lake Michigan with floor-to-ceiling windows, plush carpeting, and a décor reminiscent of a 1968 Elvis concert. Purple velvet was the theme-setting color with some Indian relics thrown in to give authenticity to the work of the management team.

The primary focus of the company was the management of the single casino owned by the tribe, the Olatagwa Casino and Convention Center, located contiguous to the Olatagwa State Park bordering Hinkley County. The Olatagwa Indian Counsel acted as a board of directors, but the day-to-day management of the casino was delegated to Lou Little Hare Luchini, hailed as an experienced executive handling all tribal affairs relating to the casino.

Since the casino was located on re-constituted reservation land, the tribe was free of all local and state regulation, as well as immune from local law enforcement. They maintained their own security force that was headed by Frank Spear Chucker Salucci, well known in the gambling community as a fearless enforcer who could sniff out a card cheat before he ever took a seat at a table. In addition to his casino security responsibilities, Frank also looked after collections when the occasional whale exceeded their credit limit. A high roller who maintained a minimum fifty thousand dollar credit limit was referred to as a whale and drew considerable attention in the casino, both accommodating and at times, when the credit ran out, distasteful. Frank could dispense distasteful like no other.

The intercom buzzed and a voice said, "Frank's here to see you, Mr. Luchini."

"Send him in." Lou slid the papers to the side of his desk. "Things better get better, Joe. That's all I got to say."

"You mean you want me to change the flop?" Joe Little Cloud said. The flop referred to the payback on the slots. A central computer that calculated the percentage of return controlled all of the machines.

"You heard me, things better get better. And I ain't talking about the economy."

The office door opened and Frank Spear Chucker stepped in. "You want to see me, boss? I'm just about ready to head back to the casino."

Lou opened a drawer and pulled out a piece of paper. "You get a chance to check out this Ray Lightfeather? He's called me ten times since I talked to you. He's gettin' on my nerves."

31

Frank pulled a paper out of his official Olatagwa Indian Casino briefcase and put on his reading glasses. "Ray Chicken Hawk Lightfeather; confirmed to be fifty-percent pure-bred Olatagwa; grew up rural Illinois with no juvenile record; moved to California and worked in the entertainment industry; had one arrest for malicious destruction of property, driving under the influence, and resisting arrest; returned to Hinkley County, Illinois, worked several jobs including owning and running a car sales lot; indicted for odometer fraud, wire fraud, title conversion but not convicted; currently receives an average of two thousand a month from the casino. That's about it. Lives alone, drives a 2007 Ford pickup; doesn't drink anymore; no known drug relationships; last known occupation shown as wholesale distribution. From what I could find out, he buys Chinese trinkets and sells them as authentic hand-made Indian relics."

Lou pulled the chewed end of the cigar out of his mouth and took a drink from a water bottle on a tray next to his desk. Then he studied the end of his cigar, getting ready to take another chomp. "Don't sound like he's much of a trouble maker. You've got a bigger rap sheet than that. He's Injun, huh? I didn't know there was any of them left. I mean, we send all those checks out every month, but most of them say they are fifth cousins, twice removed or something."

Frank stared at the wet, scraggly end of Lou's half eaten cigar, having trouble swallowing even though the cigar was in someone else's mouth. "Uh, what was it you want? I mean, what about this guy. He applying for a job or something?"

"How much does he get from us each month?" Lou asked with a frown.

Frank glanced at his notes again. "A couple thousand, depending on the casino take each month."

"Really, I didn't know we doled out that much, except for some of the political guys that helped get the reservation legislation through. Must be because he's got so much Injun, huh?" Lou leaned back in his chair, put his feet up on his desk, shoved the cigar back in his mouth, thoughtfully looked at the ceiling, and then he continued, "He's got some deal he wants to talk to me about, something about windmills to cut our electric bill at the casino. Says he can save us thousands of dollars every month. Barb says when he calls he talks like the Injuns talk in the movies. You ever talk to him?"

"Never met him. Just did the background like you asked. You want me to go talk to him? I can scare him away if you want. Threaten to cut off his checks from the casino, and maybe some other things too."

Lou's rubbery lips wrapped around the wet cigar and he continued to chew while he contemplated the proposition.

Joe Little Cloud went to the bar in the corner of the room and poured three fingers of bourbon in a tumbler. "He wants to sell us windmills? Come on, you're kidding, right? Fuck's he think we do, run a ranch with cows and chickens? That's the only place I ever seen a windmill. Yeah, in pictures with cows and chickens and on TV."

Lou didn't move or look over. "Shut up, Joe." He made the cigar move up and down like a toothpick in his mouth. "Maybe go to his house, see what he's up to, see if he's got anyone else around. If he's pure Injun, maybe he lives in a teepee or something."

"Lives in a trailer," Frank responded.

"Okay, on your way back to the casino, stop in town and have a look around, see what he's up to. Maybe he's legit." Lou pulled the cigar out of his mouth and studied the end, like he was looking for the tenderest morsel to bite off.

Frank said, trying not to look at the cigar, "I'll let you know if I find anything."

"And find out about this wind thing. If it saves us a ton of money like he says, maybe we should look at it. Hell, maybe we could do a cowboy and Injun thing like Joe said, you know, have a little amusement park with some chickens and cows for the kids and a couple windmills to power the casino, fit right in, part of the theme. We could even have an old-time saloon for the parents with a ton of slots and some craps tables. Have everyone dressed in old time get ups." Lou smiled and leaned back, studying the ceiling, chomping on the cigar with increased vigor.

Joe downed his drink and headed back to the bar. "Could even have a T and A show up on an old-time stage. It'd fit right in."

"Shut up, Joe." Lou lost his smile. "Go check it out, Frank. Bring me some good news for a change." Lou looked at Joe and said with a smirk, "Tits and ass, that's the best you can come up with, huh."

CHAPTER 5

Frank pulled into the Hinkley Motor Inn on the outskirts of town late enough in the day that there was no use starting his inquiry until the morning. The motel consisted of about fifteen rooms. Frank guessed they were 1960's vintage, all in a row with parking in front. A covered walkway went from the office on one end to the last room on the other. One other car was parked in front of a room.

Through the office door he could see some vending machines, the sparsely appointed office, and an unattended counter. A large sign hung on the lower portion of the door stating: VACANCY – NO PETS.

Stepping through the door, he noticed a lingering haze of smoke that smelled of a mixture of lilac incense and curry. This motel was either managed or owned by Middle Easterners. He could hear unintelligible arguing beyond the door behind the counter along with screams of a small child. He decided to look for another motel or just sleep in his car.

Frank's hesitation allowed time for a dark-complexioned young woman dressed in a multi-colored floor-length robe of some sort with a matching scarf tied on her head and a dot on her forehead to come to the counter, stand at attention, and ask in serious broken English, "Yes, may we give help?"

Frank had his hand on the door. "Uh, yeah, I guess. I need a room." Frank glanced toward the parking lot. "I assume you have some vacancies."

"How long for you to stay?"

Frank couldn't help but stare at the spot on the young lady's forehead. It was blue, so it had to be an intentional tattoo as opposed to a birthmark. "Just for the night," he responded. What circumstance would justify tattooing a dot on your forehead?

"Thirty dollar cash, thirty-five dollar credit. No pet."

Frank pulled out his Olatagwa Indian Reservation Casino credit card and gave it to the young lady.

She looked at the card, gave Frank a big smile that drew lines in her forehead and stretched her dot, turned, and yelled some gibberish toward the door behind the counter.

A man of equally dark complexion peeked around the door, smiled, and said, "You casino man?" He stepped up to the counter and aggressively pushed the young lady aside and behind him. "You work casino?" He smiled. "I play poker profession. Someday go Las Vegas."

"Hey, good for you." Frank said. "What room you want me to use?"

"Texas hold'um. I play Internet. Make big money. Go to Las Vegas."

This was getting annoying. The guy's smile was so bright compared to his dark skin and shiny black hair, he must have false teeth. And the stench of his breath was about to make Frank sick. The young girl was now peeking around the guy's shoulder, pointing her dot at Frank and continuing to smile. "Uh, look, I really don't care. No offense, but can I have my room key?"

The guy examined the credit card again, looked up, smiled. "You like play poker? We have Internet, I come to room, we play. Show you best place to play. Win big money."

Something popped in Frank's head. His eye began twitching and his fist clenched up with such force his forearm muscle started to spasm. He reached across the counter and grabbed the smiling Indian by the shirt and lifted him up close to his face. "Give me a fucking room key, jungle boy, and if you want to ever play poker again, don't come to my room."

The man's eyes were popping, but he continued to smile, although it did appear a little forced. He made some unintelligible sounds and the woman pulled a key from under the counter and moved it gently toward Frank's other hand. Frank slowly let the poker player slide back down until his feet touched the floor, took the key and his credit card off the counter, produced a wad of bills and threw thirty dollars down before turning and walking out.

Frank almost broke the door to the room, jamming the key and forcing it open with his shoulder. His nerves were sparking and blood pressure still peaking. He sat down on the bed and rubbed his forehead. His clean-cut appearance and mild approach were deceiving. The one thing in Frank's structured life he had trouble controlling was his temper. His tolerance for objection or lack of submission to his demand was near zero. And the eruption of displeasure was always the same. Like an electrical short circuit in his brain, it would spark and then his right eye would start twitching and his fist would involuntarily ball up.

Fortunately, the little Indian guy new better than to resist.

◆　◆　◆

Frank rose early and dined at the Kountry Kitchen just across the street from the motel. Halfway through his second cup of coffee, he asked the counter waitress, "You ever see a guy named Ray Lightfeather in here? He's a big guy, looks Indian, I mean real Indian, not motel Indian."

She bent down on one elbow and moved a big curl away from her eye, giving Frank a big smile that revealed one missing tooth among the twisted mess of enamel. Her blouse was cut low enough to show off her heart tattoo in the middle of her cleavage with the letters E.Z. above it. "I know Ray. Chew got to be careful though. You a cop?"

"No, just want to talk to him. Business. Be careful, why?"

The waitress looked around as if she was revealing some kind of secret. "Chew know, hee's kind of, I don't know, quiet. Likes to be alone. Don want nobody in hee's business."

"You must know him pretty well. What's the E. Z. stand for?" Dumb question, but she didn't seem like the brightest bulb in the pack and she seemed to know Ray.

Her pocked face brightened and the crooked smile got even bigger. "I could cho you. Where you stay?"

A fat guy with a dirty apron stuck his head out from the kitchen and yelled, "Maria, this ain't show and tell. You got orders wait'in."

Maria hesitated, rose, and adjusted her apron in front of Frank, giving a little jiggle of her protruding breasts, blew him a kiss, and headed for the kitchen.

Over the next half hour, Maria hovered over Frank's coffee cup, and between repeated questions about where he was staying and what time would he like to meet, she divulged that Ray spent much of his time in his trailer or working in a rented barn on a farm just out of town. She had been there but couldn't quite remember where, but she might be able to "cho heem," in his car, after work.

Frank passed on the guide offer and told Maria he'd be back for lunch, what year he didn't specify.

Ray's trailer was in the Placid Living Mobile Home and RV Park located next to the Wal-Mart on the south end of town. The trailer was pretty easy to locate because it had a totem pole carved from an old power pole leaning against the awning with numerous other fake artifacts scattered around the condensed yard.

Maintenance free living must have been the hallmark of this trailer's manufacturer. The appearance indicated there hadn't been any maintenance for a long time. Ray's pickup was nowhere in sight, but Frank made the gesture of knocking on the steel door so he could look in the window. No one answered. Frank's attempt to open the door was stymied by a deadbolt lock. A cat meandered out from under the trailer and sniffed Frank's polished shoe, rubbed up against his cuff, and then went back under the trailer, apparently satisfied he was not delivering any food.

Someone slid a window open in the next trailer and a voice, coarse and deep with an accompanying smoker rasp, said, "Ain't home." There were a few coughs and then, "What chew want? You got a badge? I seen you try to open the door. I tell Ray, he kick you ass, I ain't ly'in. What chew want?"

Frank could only see a silhouette in the window behind a screen. "County tax agent. Checking on owners, see if these are rented. Changes the tax. So, you're telling me Ray Lightfeather lives here. That checks out. You rent?"

The window slammed shut.

Trying to find the rented barn wouldn't be so easy unless he wanted to wrestle Maria in the back seat of his car, which would be filed under last resort.

The best place to get information in a small town was the local bar, so he made a slow drive on the main street and found Ralphy's, a storefront bar with the front door propped open. He wandered in and took a seat, looking around the dark, empty room; expected, at only nine o'clock in the morning. Two guys in bib overalls and ball caps sat at the other end of the room drinking coffee. No one was behind the bar.

One of the men drinking coffee turned and looked at Frank, turned back to the other, and made an indistinguishable remark and turned again. "You want a coffee? The cups are there behind the bar and the pot's next the cash register. Help yourself. That's the way we do it around here. Ralphy's downstairs chasin' rats or something. You want something stronger, you'll have to wait 'til he gets done." The guy returned to his muffled conversation.

Frank went around the bar and retrieved his coffee, stood stirring it, and then moseyed down the bar to the boys in the bibs. He waited for a break in their conversation, which didn't take long when he stopped next to them. "You boys from around here?"

They both looked at him from under their ball-cap bills without reply.

"I'll take that as a yes. I'm trying to locate a guy named Ray Lightfeather. He sells Indian relics and such and I'm a dealer. You know him? Maybe know where he stores his stuff?"

The two guys looked at each other without expression and the bigger of the two responded, "None of my business where he keeps his stuff. Don't suppose it's none of yourn neither."

The other guy pulled on his cap, like he was trying to squeeze out a thought. "Ray ain't too friendly. I mean, he don't talk much. He was in the movies, you know. He told me once, he got kilt in something like twenty movies. He's an Olatagwa, you know. His momma was breed. My old man said she was a looker too." He smiled at his friend. "Wore those leather pants, you know, before they was popular like you see in *Penthouse* now. He always talked about her. She lived out on an acre plot off of Coldwater road, you know. Grew herbs and such. Probably some wacky weed too, you know."

"That place have a barn?" Frank asked.

The big guy frowned and gave the talker a squint that answered Frank's question.

"Don't matter," Frank said. "I'm not interested in herbs." Frank set his cup on the bar, pulled out a dollar bill, and laid it there as well. "Nice talkin' to you gentlemen. If you see Ray, just tell him he's got a customer looking for him. I'm sure he'll find me if he wants to." Frank turned and walked out, thinking about finding a gas station attendant to ask how to find Coldwater road.

Chapter 6

Coldwater Road was not much more than a gravel path once you rounded the first curve away from the main highway. It meandered along the hilly divide that identified the Olatagwa River basin with an occasional country home hidden among the trees, some working farms with some livestock browsing in the fields, and a lot of no trespassing signs. So far, no sign of a stand-alone barn or Ray's pickup truck.

Crossing a culvert bridge and rounding another blind corner, Frank came upon what appeared to be an abandoned house, overgrown with thicket and vines, two junk cars in the yard with parts spread around, a pile of garbage bags spilling into a ditch, and an old dilapidated barn set back among a spread of overgrown spruce trees. Tire tracks led from the road to the barn but no working vehicles were in sight.

Frank sat in his car picturing the house and barn when once occupied, an Indian princess pruning flowers or gathering herbs. Now the porch leaned near collapse, all of the windows broken or missing and vegetation nearly enveloped one side growing up the cracked chimney. The barn looked in similar condition, although it appeared structurally sound. The lone window was still in place and a no-trespassing sign was displayed on the double barn door. Still, the placid scene gave no hint of any human activity. The tire tracks leading to the barn were fresh enough to convince Frank the barn was being used. He stepped out of the car, leaned against the door, and continued to take in the surroundings.

◆ ◆ ◆

Ray knelt underneath a big sycamore tree about one hundred yards behind the barn on top of a rise, giving a panoramic perspective of the house, barn, and road. The car was not familiar and when the man got out and continued to inspect the property, he was not familiar either. The guy looked like a cop but the car didn't fit the profile with its spoke wheels and polished finish. He seemed to be plenty patient, not making any moves, just leaning against the car. Ray could be patient too, pulling a piece of jerky out of his pouch and gnawing off a chunk.

Ray spent the morning looking for mushrooms and deer sheds, both unsuccessful. The man in the car was an interruption because he wanted to be back at the trailer by 11 to see *The Price Is Right*, but he could wait. One day he'd return to Hollywood and make it to the final spin for the showcase. His arm around Drew Carey, he'd win the fantastic array of kitchen appliances or the new car or boat. Telling Drew that he was in over twenty movies and had eaten dinner at Jay Silverheel's house. Spent the evening watching *Lone Ranger* serials and drinking hundred-dollar-a-bottle firewater.

The man moved around the car and started walking up the rutted driveway toward the barn. Stopped, checked the mud on his shoes, and changed his mind.

Good. Turn around and go back where you came from.

♦ ♦ ♦

Frank looked down at his shoes that were sinking into the soft soil while the mud seeped over onto his socks. The Florsheims were brand new and now they looked like he worked on a farm. He pulled up his pant legs and hopped back to the car and the harder road surface. Searching the trunk of the car, he found a towel and diligently wiped the shoes clean, took off his socks, put them in a bag, threw it in the trunk, and climbed into the car.

Getting close to noon, nearly ruined a new pair of shoes, and he didn't even know if this was Ray's hideout. There was no way to run surveillance on the place without camping in the woods, and besides, none of this was important enough to endure the inconvenience of sitting for hours waiting for someone who may never show. He looked down at his bare feet. Might as well go back to town and nose around some more. Maybe Ray would show up for lunch or dinner at the Kountry Kitchen for a rendezvous with Maria. Frank reached for the ignition.

"You lost or somethin'?"

Frank looked in his side rear view mirror and all he could see was a big belt buckle.

"Nobody lives here, so what you want."

This was a big guy but the voice sounded like a child. Frank slowly opened the car door, letting the guy know he was making a move and then realized not having on any shoes or socks might look a little strange. So he leaned out and looked back at Ray. "In real estate, just checking some of the properties out here. You own it? Got my feet all muddy in the drive. Interested in selling?"

Ray didn't respond, his big Stetson blocking the morning sun.

Frank took in the countenance of the man. Had to be six five or better. Older, but in good shape. Features that are unmistakably Indian. "Nice place, I mean, a young couple might be interested as a fixer upper, you know what I mean. Could probably get you a good price, that is, if it's yours." Frank reached over and grabbed his shoes, pulled the keys from the ignition, deciding to get out and engage Ray in some conversation, get this investigation back on track. He swung the door open and struggling to get the shoes on his bare feet, looked up, and Ray was gone. The shoes only half on, Frank got out and saw Ray crossing a ditch and walking back into the woods.

"Hey, what about the place? How about giving me a call?" Frank turned and got back into the car. "Stupid Indian."

CHAPTER 7

Harold sat at his desk, looking at a pile of bills in his "IN" basket. Saturday, normally his busiest day of the week, two customers so far and neither purchased anything. Joe Burris needed a steel washer, a two-cent item that Harold did not have in stock, and Bud Runyan wanted to know if his five-year-old lawn mower was still under warranty because it wouldn't start.

Ray Lightfeather's card leaned against the desk lamp and Harold picked it up and rubbed the raised gold lettering. Suppose Ray was serious? He was Indian and the casino was run by Indians, maybe he did have an in with all that money, something about his uncle.

Harold picked up the phone and dialed.

The phone engaged but no one spoke.

"Ray?" Harold asked.

"Who wants to know?"

"Uh, it's Harold, Harold Hanover, the hardware store?"

"Chicken Hawk busy."

"Uh, yeah, sorry to bother you Mister, uh, Hawk." Harold sighed, this was probably a big mistake. "You still interested in the turbines? You know, you asked about wind turbines last week."

"What you find out?"

"Well, I didn't find out a lot, I mean, I guess I just want to know if you are still interested. Maybe we could partner up on this thing. I can get this stuff wholesale, you know, save you, uh, us, some big bucks."

"Chicken Hawk don't need no partner. How much they cost, these tur-bines, wholesale?"

Now he'd stepped in it. Ray'd want everything at Harold's cost. "I'll have to get back to you on that, but, you know, if we work together on this."

"Yeah, you get back to Chicken Hawk." The phone made the monotonous disconnect sound.

Stupid Indian.

43

♦ ♦ ♦

Nub pushed open the door and the hanging bell tinkled. He walked up to the cashier counter and waited while Mr. Hanover finished his telephone call. By standing on his tiptoes, he was just tall enough to see over the counter. "Hi, Mr. Hanover."

"Oh, hi, Nub. You're not looking for more of that computer stuff are you? I still don't have any. Your daddy send you in?"

Nub pulled a paper out of his shorts and put it on the counter. "Can you check on this stuff? It's for a science project."

Harold pushed back from the desk, and came over to the counter, pulling his reading glasses out of his pocket for his one good eye. "Okay, what we got here, Nub? What kind of science we dealing with, stainless-steel screws and nuts? Stainless dowel pin with a tinsel strength of eight hundred-foot pounds per … Who gave you this? What's this for? Waterproof, non-acidic lubricating compound… What the heck you doin', Nub, buildin' a bomb?" Harold looked up from the paper and over his glasses, eyebrows raised. "You're not, are you?"

"Come on, Mr. Hanover, why would I build a bomb. You can buy those on the Internet any time you want. I'm building a wind turbine. Well, actually, not a turbine like, you know, you see on TV, but a generator powered by wind for the farm. You heard about the guy who took all the money?"

"Uh, yeah, I read something about that in the paper, I guess." He returned to studying the list.

"Well, since he ain't gonna do it, I figure with a little scroungin' around, I can put something together that's just as good. I found a diesel generator over at Bud's salvage yard that the motor is burnt up but the generator still looks good, so I traded a feeder that I got to butcher and wrap for him even-Steven. I just got to haul the thing home."

"Whoa," Harold said, "wait a minute, you think you can build a wind turbine from scratch? Come on, Nub, these things are complicated."

"I found an issue of *Popular Mechanics* that gives a general plan for a home wind generator. I'm using that to make my own design. The biggest problem I have is the propeller, the thing that catches the wind. Well, it's actually not a propeller, like you would see on a plane. They're actually designed to –"

Harold held up his hands. "Hold on, Nub. I've seen these things on TV, they're complicated, I mean, some of 'em are what, hundreds of feet high. It's not some whirly-gig like you wear on your hat or stick in the garden to shoo away birds." Harold gave Nub a patronizing smile. "Now, why don't you just reach in the old candy bowl and grab a handful and forget all this nonsense."

Nub, his cheeks burnished from the anger, pushed the paper list toward Harold and said slowly, "You got this stuff, or not?"

"Now, Nub, don't get all huffy." Harold leaned on his elbow against the counter and studied the list. "What's this E-10 capacitor? Like I told you before, I don't carry all of this fancy computer stuff. And the stainless, that stuff's expensive, Nub."

"You want a pig? I'll butcher it and even wrap it. Chops, fresh side, ribs, you name it."

CHAPTER 8

Ray Lightfeather sat in a big overstuffed lounge chair in his trailer and leafed through a *National Geographic* magazine he had borrowed from the Library looking for the article titled, "Wind, The Future Is Now." In addition to several borrowed magazines, he had printed off federal tax guidelines for energy tax credits for green energy projects, a list of companies that supply wind turbines in the mid-west, and borrowed a book titled, *The Complete Guide To Wind Powered Energy.*

He had called the business office of the casino in Chicago and was told Mr. Luchini was busy and would get back to him. He had heard that song and dance before, so he called his uncle, Lance Thrustworthy, head of maintenance at the casino.

"Lance, this is Ray, you heard anything?"

"*About what?*" Lance responded.

"About the wind turbines. You said you would talk to your boss about it." Even though Lance was his uncle by marriage to his mother's younger sister, they were about the same age and had been close, at least until the car Ray sold him with a lifetime warranty blew up. But that was another story.

"Yeah, I mentioned it, gave 'em your card like you said. The guy that's head of security said he would check it out."

"What the guy look like?" A light bulb went off in Ray's head.

"Good lookin' guy. I think he was military or something, always dresses like he just stepped out of a magazine, you know what I mean? Frank, Frank Salucci. Get this, you know what they call him around here? Spear Chucker. I'm serious, all these Italian guys that run this place tried to make up Indian names for themselves. His is Spear Chucker. Can you believe that? The big boss grease-ball's name is Little Cloud or something."

"Okay, I think I met him. So, you think they might go for this?"

"Don't know," Lance responded. "They once bought a robot floor-cleaning machine because the salesman said it would eliminate one janitor. One night it caused thirty thousand dollars damage to a bunch of slot machines before anyone could shut it off. It's sitting in the basement storage room now. They bought an automatic drink-dispensing machine that pre-mixed stuff, you know, hoping to eliminate a barmaid. Trouble was, all the customers complained because every drink tasted the same, no matter what was in it. So the bar business went into the toilet and the drink-dispensing machine is sitting next to the floor-cleaning robot.

"So, do I think they will buy into your wind-machine scam, sure, why not? Anyone that would name themselves Spear Chucker or Little Cloud can't be all that smart."

"It *ain't* a scam." Ray hesitated then realized Lance's opinion wasn't going to matter anyway. "So, I guess I should talk to this Frank guy, or Spear Chucker. His office at the casino?"

◆　◆　◆

Frank sat at the counter of the Kountry Kitchen sipping his coffee that had been topped off three times by Maria. Since he sat down, she had systematically unbuttoned two more notches of her blouse, giving a more picturesque view of her heart and E.Z. tattoo and immense cleavage. Getting Ray's telephone number without contacting a sexually transmitted disease seemed to be a long shot, but worth a try.

Maria rested an elbow on the counter in front of Frank and blinked. "Chew want anything to eat? The especial today is meatloaf. I get off at 3."

Frank gave her his charmed look and asked whimsically, "What am I going to do for two hours. You know, I could try to call—"

"Chew want to go out back?" Maria said, her eyes bright with excitement. "I could take my break now."

"Uh, no, but while I'm waiting, maybe I could call Ray Lightfeather. You have his number?"

All twenty of Maria's remaining brain cells seemed to focus on the question and whether to give up what little leverage she had on the handsome suitor. "Chew going to wait for me, 'til 3?"

Frank gave her a big smile.

Maria walked to the other end of the counter and searched through her handbag, pulled out a cell phone, and winked at Frank while she punched numbers. "Don know if hee's home." She held the phone to her ear. "Ray, you there?...Yeah, it's Marie... How you do, babe?... Meatloaf, you coming in?... Guy here want to talk to you...Yeah, kinda." Marie put her hand over the phone and smiled. "He ax if you es good looking." She listened again. "He ax es you the real estate guy?"

Frank's head was buzzing. He was about to tear the phone out of Maria's hand, slap her upside the head, and walk outside.

Just in time, the cook looked around the wall and yelled, "Marie, get your wetback ass in here and pick up these orders." Then he saw the cell phone. "I told you, one more time on that phone and you were done."

Frank yanked the phone from Maria's hand and waved at the cook. "Sorry, my phone. Go on, hon, deliver your meatloaf." Frank stood and walked from the counter. "Ray, you still there?"

"Who wants to know?"

"My name's Frank, work for the casino, I need to talk to you." Frank waited for a reply.

"What about? I thought you sold real estate."

"Yeah, well, I do that too. You got time to meet?"

"Meet at hardware store. Three o'clock."

"Okay, I can do... Ray, you still... Hello." Frank looked at the phone. "Stupid Indian."

CHAPTER 9

Harold busied himself by sorting through the store's nuts and bolts inventory, rooting out the wrong sizes misplaced by customers. It had been another day without the cash register ringing up a sale. He tried to focus on the task, comparing the sizes of the screws as he surveyed each drawer, but his attention span was weak and the gnawing gurgle of what he suspected to be a bleeding ulcer pinched under his ribs.

How could he let a low-life carnival huckster get to him so easily? The thought never left and he had not slept through a night since the guy disappeared. Worse than that, the chip on his wife's shoulder had turned into a whole log and was about to weigh down their forty-year marriage.

The hardware store had not turned over enough cash the past few weeks to pay the power bill, or any other bill for that matter. Hopefully, Ray Lightfeather would generate some kind of miracle deal that would turn things around, but his most recent calls had gone unanswered and he still was in the dark about where to find the type of equipment Ray had asked about.

Harold retreated to his desk and swallowed a big gob of pink Pepto-Bismol.

The doorbell tinkled and a well-dressed stranger with TV star stature, and looks to match, wandered around the front of the store, sizing up the inventory but seeming to keep an eye on the front window, as if surveillance of the street was of greater priority than buying hardware.

Harold took the initiative from behind the counter. "Good afternoon." The greeting drew the man's attention but he turned back to the window. "Anything I can show you? Need any help? We got most anything to do with the home. Don't know I've seen you around before. New in town?"

The man finally turned and replied, "Just looking around. I'll let you know if I need anything."

Harold shuffled a couple papers on his desk, opened and closed the cash drawer, moved the candy dish a little on the counter, and walked toward the customer.

"That Toro will mow until you are too old to walk behind it, I'll guarantee that. Got a heck of deal goin' today too. Get you six months same as cash, you need it." Harold leaned against an end-cap.

The customer continued to stare at the front window.

Harold continued, "You new in town?"

The customer turned and sighed. "You know Ray Lightfeather?"

The guy looked like a cop. Answering in the affirmative could get him involved with Ray, known for some slick deals. "Yeah, I mean, he's an occasional customer, tools and stuff, I mean, not like burglary tools or anything like that."

This drew the guy's attention and he cocked his head. "What do you mean, burglary tools? Why would he buy burglary tools?"

"No, no, I said he wouldn't buy that kind of stuff." Heartburn tickled the back of Harold's throat. "He was a movie star, you know that? At least, that's what I heard. He's part Olatagwa Indian. That's about all I know, I mean, I really don't know him much, other than as a customer, buying tools and such." Harold couldn't help himself. He had to ask. "You looking for him? He in trouble or something?"

The guy resumed his surveillance of the street.

"You with the police or something? My brother-in-law's the sheriff here, maybe he could help." Harold had his back to the door and heard the bell tinkle. He turned and was looking at Ray Lightfeather's chest, Ray standing a full head taller than Harold.

Ray stood silent and crossed his arms over his elk-horn-buttoned leather vest, the leather giving a slight squeak from the pressure.

"Hey Ray," Harold mumbled. "This here's..." Harold looked at the other guy. "This here gentleman is, kind of, looking for you."

Harold rubbed his chin, trying to keep his hand from shaking while the two men stared at one another in silence, the only sound that of the fluorescent light humming above them.

The good-looking guy looked at Harold and said without emotion, "Ray and I need to talk, *alone*."

Harold took the queue and gladly started for the back room.

Ray said, "He stay. He my supplier, get tur-bines."

Harold stopped and gulped back some bile.

The guy's eyebrow raised a notch. "Thought you didn't know him."

"Uh, well, I didn't say that. I said he was a customer, I mean, tools and stuff... and maybe wind turbines."

"Okay, my name's Frank Salucci." He looked at Harold and then Ray. "That's what I want talk about Ray, this windmill thing. You been calling my boss about selling windmills to the casino."

"Chicken Hawk make deal," Ray tilted his head at Harold, "he get machines."

Frank rubbed his face in frustration. "What's with the broken English? You retarded or something? This isn't some cowboy and Indian movie. What's with this town anyway, is it the water?" Frank shook his head and turned to Harold. "Okay, so you are going to supply the windmills. Where you getting 'em?"

Harold coughed into his hand, looked at Ray for help but knew it wasn't coming. "Well, there are several vendors we are in negotiation with. There are so many variables we have to consider... and that will certainly influence our decision." Harold belched under his breath, swallowed, trying to keep from throwing up and concentrate so his hands would not shake.

"Humor me. Give me the name of one of the vendors," Frank said, crossing his arms.

Ray was still standing with his arms crossed as well, his dark eyes and pursed lips adding to a stern expression that would have made Geronimo proud.

Harold's fake eye was bulging and sweat started to bead on his forehead. "Well, I, uh, I don't think it would be prudent at this point to identify our suppliers. You know, these things are highly complicated, they're full of stainless steel, stuff like dowel pins with, I don't know, hundreds of pounds of tin, tin, tinkle strength. They're full of E-10 capacitors and use special lube acid, stuff like that. You just can't find manufacturers around every corner."

Frank stared at Harold without comment for what seemed like ten minutes before saying, "You know what tripe is ...? What's your name?"

"Harold, Harold Hanover."

"You know what tripe is, *Harold*?"

Harold started to open his mouth, Frank cut him off. "Tripe is the only part of a cow that's worth less than what comes out of its butt. What I just heard is a bunch of tripe, Harold." Frank looked at Ray. "You have anything to add?"

"Wind tur-bines save big money. Casino use much electricity."

Frank shook his head. "Seriously, what's with the Injun talk? You get hit in the head or something? Okay, I've heard enough." Frank continued to shake his head as he headed for the front door. Holding the door open, he said before exiting, "You guys make a great act, you know it? Maybe some day they'll do a re-make of *Dumb and Dumber.*"

Chapter 10

HINKLEY MESSENGER
By-line: Red Redderson, Editor
OLATAGWA CASINO BETS ON WIND

The Olatagwa Indian Casino, located in Hinkley County Illinois, and its Counsel of Indian Affairs, in a written statement announced Monday that they are adopting a clean- energy plan that includes installation of 3 wind-driven electricity generators capable of producing enough electricity to reduce conventional power consumption by 10%. The casino entered into a 10-year agreement with Clean-Air Systems LTD of Modesto, California to erect and maintain the generators. The statement did not identify the exact location where the generators will be erected other than to say it will be on the reservation within proximity of the casino.

Although the cost of the project was not announced, the Department of Energy, through its Clean Energy Grant Program, is providing a two million dollar tax credit to the casino. The casino is located on the Olatagwa Indian Reservation and is not subject to federal tax laws. Calls to the Olatagwa Casino offices and the Olatagwa Indian Affairs Counsel Offices regarding use of the tax credits went unanswered. Through the Freedom Of Information Act, The Messenger was able to secure a copy of the grant filing that identified the recipient of the tax credit to be Little Hair Leasing LTD, the company that will lease the generators to the casino. The President of Little Hair Leasing LTD is Cecilia Luchini, wife of the Chief Operating Officer of the Olatagwa Casino, Louigi Luchini.

The statement offered an estimated project-completion date as last quarter of this year. Harold Hanover, President of the Hinkley County Chamber of Commerce, would not comment on the project other than to say, "As a member of the Chamber, I am sorely disappointed that the casino management contracted with an out-of-state firm."

♦ ♦ ♦

Frank sat in a plush couch across from a large mahogany conference table watching Lou Luchini study a topography map of the Indian Reservation. Joe Little Cloud Rondelo clinked ice cubes into a glass at the office bar.

"So, Frank," Joe said while they waited for Lou to complete his study of the map, "that Mex you told me about, the one with the tattoo, you think she's still at that diner? I got to go to the casino this week. I might stop there for lunch, if you know what I mean."

Frank watched Lou study the map and replied without looking at Rondelo, "No idea, but if she is, I'm sure she will be happy to show you the daily special, bugs and all."

Lou cocked his head and leaned closer to the map. "Dis spot here, it looks like the highest spot on the map. Frank, look at this, is that right? And what's this mean, this squiggly thing?"

Frank had doctored the map in advance of the meeting, highlighting the area occupied by the casino and marking in red the parking lots and road right of way. He moved closer to the map and studied where Lou had his finger, what looked to be a few hundred yards from the casino. Then he looked at the map legend on the corner, noting that the squiggly thing identified the Indian burial mound on the reservation. "That's the burial mound, or serpent mound, depending on what archeologist you talk to. Remember, the original casino plan had to be moved so the construction didn't disturb the mound. It's some kind of sacred spot for the tribe."

"The *tribe*," Lou said with a laugh. "Like there's a tribe that cares who's buried there. All they care about is that the checks get mailed on the first and don't take more than a day to get to 'em. There ain't one of 'em could show real proof they're Injun."

"Oh, there's one all right," Frank said with a smirk. "The guy I checked out, you know, the one wanted to sell you the windmills. He's Injun all right, I mean, who knows what kind, but he's one-hundred-percent Injun."

"How you know," Joe asked with a chuckle, "he wear feathers and carry a tommy-hawk?"

"You screw with the Mex, you may find out. I think they're pretty close." Frank went back to the couch. "So, Mr. Luchini, you decide where to put the windmills?"

"The consultant from Clean-Air Systems said because there is so much forestation," Lou looked at Rondelo, "that means trees, No-neck. There're so many trees around the casino, the turbines have to go on the highest ground. That would be the spot I just showed you." Lou bent down again and squinted at the squiggly icon. "Right where the squiggly thing is, that's the highest ground."

Frank rubbed his chin. "That may not fly with the Council."

Lou went to his desk and pulled a large cigar from the humidor and shoved it into his mouth. "Fuck do I care what they think. You ever seen an Injun, or for that matter, anyone that had to decide between a big pile of money or saving a hill where maybe someone they don't even know might be buried, turn down the money? Ain't gonna happen. Remember when a bunch of 'em got upset because we turned the artifacts room at the casino into a private high-stakes blackjack parlor? As soon as Chief Morningstar saw that Cadillac in his driveway, there wasn't another word said. He didn't even ask what happened to the junk that was in there." Lou chewed some of the cigar and swallowed. "By the way, Joe, what happened to all that stuff? There was a bunch of arrowheads, rocks, some feather hats…Where'd it all go?"

Joe looked at Frank without turning his head, a veil of guilt shrouding his face, and then looked at Lou who waited for an answer. "Uh, I'll have to look into that."

Lou chewed another inch off his cigar and said, "How much you get for 'em?"

Now Frank's interest was spurred. "You sell the stuff, Joe? Mr. Luchini asked you a question."

Joe put his finger to his chin and looked at the ceiling. "That's been a while ago. I'd have to go back and check the records. But I'll get back to you, don't *you worry*. I'll find out what happened to that stuff, and believe me, *someone* will hear about it!" Joe started to get up to leave.

Lou pulled the half-eaten cigar from his mouth, looked at it as if at a half eaten O'Henry chocolate bar, and said without emotion, "Sit down, Joe."

Joe slowly let himself back on the couch. The silence in the room was only interrupted by Lou's raspy breathing.

Lou licked his lips, snagging an errant tobacco stem and swallowed. "So," he let the beginning comment linger, "you sold the stuff, eh? How much you get?"

Joe wiggled a little and pulled at his open shirt collar that partially covered his cheeks. Then he looked at the ceiling again as if he was trying to remember the transaction. "Boy, that's been a while ago, you know. Let's see, we may have sent that stuff to the auction. Yeah, that might be what happened, we sent it to the auction."

"Who's this *we* you're talking about?" Lou asked. "You got a partner in this scam? I've know'd you a long time, No-neck, and I can smell one of your dirty deals like it's yesterday's chicken salad. How much you get, you little whack-off?"

Joe squirmed some more, beady eyes darting between Lou and Frank. "'Bout thirty grand."

"Is that 'bout closer to thirty or is it closer to forty?" Lou shoved the cigar back in his mouth and chewed.

"Maybe forty, give or take."

Frank finally spoke up. "Sounds a lot more like take than give."

Lou pulled the cigar out of his mouth and said, "Ain't that the truth." He scooted from the desk and leaned back in the chair examining the half-eaten cigar. "Seems to me, we got some squarin' up to do. What you think, Frank."

"I'd say he got a little greedy."

Joe started to open his mouth.

Lou held up his hand. "I think you've said enough. The verdict is in and the jury has spoken. Since you decided to be such a greedy little fucker, tomorrow I want two bags of cash, one on my desk and one on Frank's. Thirty thousand for me and ten thousand for Frank." Lou pointed his fingers that held the cigar at Joe. "And if I find out one penny of it came out of the casino, you'll end up as cattle feed, you understand?"

Joe swallowed hard, looked at Lou and Frank, smiled weakly, and said, "I could use a drink. Get you guys anything?"

Chapter 11

Nub fiddled with a flywheel at the top of an eighteen-foot section of used antenna stanchion he had salvaged from Elmer's TV and Appliance. The antenna stanchion had only cost Nub a fresh ham and the promise of a suckling pig to have it delivered.

His dad steadied the ladder. "Nub, I still don't see how this is gonna work."

Nub didn't pay any attention as he adjusted the flywheel and belt that turned the gear attached to the drive shaft that ran the length of the stanchion. The drive shaft attached to a transmission that turned the generator sitting on blocks on the ground. To finish the construction, Nub had to mount the propeller, an unsolved problem he was still considering.

"He make this windmill himself?" Ray Lightfeather asked, standing behind Roger.

"Son of a ... You about made me jump out of my shorts, Ray. Where'd you come from? What is this, some kind of Indian trick or something, sneaking up on me like that?"

Ray looked up at Nub on the ladder. "Smart kid, eh? I heard he was building his own windmill. Where he learn how to do that?"

"Don't know, Ray. Somehow he got a whole bunch of brains and he's always trying to use 'em. Trouble is, he ain't much on raisin' pigs, that's for sure."

Nub inched his way down the ladder. As he reached the ground, he glanced at Ray, but then turned and walked toward the barn without even a hello.

His dad said, "Nub, get *back* here. Ray here wants to talk to you. You don't just walk by somebody and not even say hi. Good Lord, son, where's your manners?" Roger looked at Ray and shook his head. "Sorry, sometimes he's just, I don't know, he just ain't too sociable, if you know what I mean."

Ray crossed his arms, gave Nub a smile. Nub scuffed his feet looking at the ground. He held a crescent wrench in his greasy hand that was about as big as his arm. Nub still did not say anything, trying to cross his arms imitating Ray, but the crescent wrench got in the way so he just stood there.

The standoff lasted a few seconds and then Ray said, "How you figure out how to do this; build this wind thing?"

"Internet and some magazines. It ain't that hard. But don't figure on stealing any of my stuff. I had to scrounge for a month to find this stuff. It ain't that easy to find."

"Nub, watch your mouth. Ray ain't gonna steal nothin'." His dad sighed and wiped his brow with a checkered handkerchief.

"The casino's building three big wind tur-bines on the reservation. You know that?" Ray knelt down and took off his Stetson, getting closer to eye level with Nub.

Nub looked at his dad and then responded, "Didn't know. I thought the guy that was selling those things stole everybody's money." Nub looked at Ray's dark face, high cheekbones, broad nose, and black braided hair. "You an Indian? I mean, a real Indian, an Olatagwa?"

Ray smiled, a golden incisor glinting in the sun. "Yeah, my mother was one of the last pure descendents. She's gone now, so I fall into that category of half-breed. You've probably heard that expression in the cowboy and Indian movies."

"Nub," his dad said, "Ray was in the movies. How many movies you been in, Ray? Cowboy movies, Nub... How many, Ray?"

Ray smiled again. "There were a lot of them. I've been killed by a cowboy about every way you could think of, shot off horses, run over by wagons, you name it, I been kilt by it."

"You the guy everyone talks about that was in the movies, in Hollywood?" Nub rubbed some grease on his shorts.

"Yeah, I even met the Lone Ranger."

"Who?" Nub frowned.

"Uh, never mind, that was a long time ago. Nub, how would you like to go look at the construction site on the reservation, where they are building the tur-bines?" Ray looked up at dad who just shrugged.

"You want to go with Ray? You won't be gone too long will you, Ray? Mom's back from Cougar Falls about 4, and she wouldn't take too kindly to Nub not bein' here."

"Yeah, I'd like to see that," Nub said.

"My truck's around the barn. Come on, Nub, let's take a ride."

♦　♦　♦

They bounced along the scrabble road in silence, heading for the four-lane. Ray finally spoke up. "Known your daddy a long time. Watched him play football in high school. He could run like the wind with that ball in his hand."

"Who's the Lone Ranger?"

Ray smiled, staring ahead down the road. Conversation with Nub wasn't going to be easy. "The Lone Ranger was a character on the radio and then on television. This was a long time ago. I never was in any of the shows, it was before my time, but I met the actor that played the Lone Ranger. His name was Clayton Moore. And he had an Indian friend named Tonto played by Jay Silverheels. I got to know Mr. Silverheels when I was in Hollywood and he introduced me to Clayton Moore, the Lone Ranger."

"Why did you go to Hollywood?"

"When I was young, well, a little older than you, the people around here didn't take too kindly to people that looked different. No matter how I dressed or cut my hair, I still looked different. I wasn't allowed to play on the football team or do stuff the other kids did so I spent most of my time in the woods or helping my mom with her farm. I never finished high school." Ray looked at Nub. "I should'a done that, finished my school. Anyway, they was makin' a whole bunch of western movies then and I saw in this magazine that extras, that's people in movies that don't say nothin', just get shot and stuff, were needed, especially if you looked Indian. So I hitchhiked to California and started going to these different studios dressed up like an old-time Indian and they started using me in their movies. You get to know the right people, you could get work pretty steady, and it paid good.

"Funny, after people around here found out I was in California and in the movies, when I'd come home, all of a sudden I wasn't different anymore, they all wanted to be my friend."

"Maybe I should get in the movies," Nub remarked, staring out the side window.

"My grandpa, he was a great Shaman of the Olatagwa, he used to tell me, about when I was your age, 'O'jujuwa,' that's what he called me. It means 'One of clean spirit..' He would say, 'O'jujuwa, only you can see what is inside, they only see what is outside.' Nub, you have much inside, more than most, so use it wisely."

Ray turned onto the reservation under a great arching sign announcing the Olatagwa Casino. As they wound up the road, the sprawling building came into view surrounded by meticulously manicured landscaping leading to acres of parking lots. The building rose several stories with a dazzling array of neon and flashing lights and a huge video screen flashing smiling faces of big winners interspersed with billings of coming events. Even though it was mid-day, there were hundreds of parked cars and people briskly walking in and out of the main entrance.

Nub's eyes widened and he sat up, hands on the door, taking in the audacious display of signage and lights as Ray took the service drive around the building. As they rounded a turn near the rear of the building, the sights changed dramatically; no more false fronts or expensive landscaping, just austere cement blocks and loading docks.

About two hundred yards away from the building and the asphalt service drive, a distinct rise in the typography gave way to an area barren of trees or shrubbery. Numerous workmen, several large trucks, and a crane now occupied the once serene area of mowed grass.

Ray parked a good distance away and watched as the workmen busied themselves, readying a large component of one of the wind-turbine stanchions to be hoisted into position.

After a few moments of silence, Ray said in a quiet voice, "They are building the tur-bines on sacred ground. It is the burial ground of my ancestors. The Ancients brought their dead to the high ground, to help lift the spirit. They would build a spire hammock and place their loved one on the high ground. Once the spirit had gone, they would burn the spire and bury the remains along with their possessions. First, the white man came and stole all the relics and now they build windmills to make their lights flash and their bells ring."

Ray leaned back in the seat. "They are building three of those things. They will be almost fifty feet high with giant propellers. It will fit right into the circus, people probably won't even notice, too busy hoping to be rich while they lose their social-security check."

"I've read about these," Nub said. "They are the Ectalon Series III. In tandem, and at full capacity, they can create twenty thousand watts of power, enough electricity to run about twenty-five normal homes. They're completely computer controlled. Wind velocity is controlled by electronically manipulating the curve of the blade to sustain maximum propulsion. A lot like an airplane with propellers. The pitch of the prop determines the propulsion. It's the problem I have with mine. I can't control the pitch, so I had to use gears and a clutch to keep the momentum from tearing everything apart."

Ray stared at Nub in astonishment. The kid had gone from wondering who the Lone Ranger was to spewing facts relating to quantum physics!

"They had to position the blades high enough to avoid the wind block of the casino building," Nub continued, straining to look around. "Every place else would have been too low. Sorry about the sacred ground. That is kind of crummy. I've been with my mom out to where my grandma is buried. It wouldn't seem right having one of these things right next to her, I mean, she probably wouldn't know it, but it still don't seem right."

Ray started the truck and turned to see where he was backing. "No, it just don't seem right."

CHAPTER 12

Hinkley County Sheriff Reginald Minor slathered another layer of butter on his pancakes as Maria Martinez refilled his coffee cup.

"Chew want anything else?" Maria bent down, exposing her EZ tattoo, and smiled.

"I know I asked you this before, but why would anyone stick a tattoo right in the middle of those things. It kind of throws off the view, you know what I mean? It's kind of like lookin' at the Grand Canyon and you got a big billboard stuck right in the middle of the view." Minor stuck another wad of pancake in his mouth and chewed, holding his fork up like he was still considering the statement.

Maria stood up, tilted her head a little to the right, tried to look down at her tattoo, like she was confirming it was still there, and finally walked away.

Minor's cell phone chirped, so he put his fork down and answered, "I'm eatin' breakfast, this better be important."

Marge Stopher, the sheriff office dispatcher, replied, "Somebody from the casino called and said there's a guy bothering people at the entrance gate. He's not on the reservation, so they can't do anything with their own security. You want me to send a cruiser? Al's clear on the other side of the county taking a theft report, somebody stole Josh Joseph's four-wheeler and ran it in the crick."

"What's the guy doin'?"

"Didn't say. Just said he's botherin' customers."

Minor looked at his half-eaten pancakes and sighed. "Okay, I'll run out there in a few minutes. Guy can't even have a peaceful breakfast anymore."

"Ain't supposed to eat breakfast at ten o'clock anyway." Marge chuckled and hung up.

♦ ♦ ♦

Ray Lightfeather stood in the middle of the two-lane entrance road, just outside and under the large looping sign announcing the casino, wearing full war paint, leather patches around his waist that barely covered what was important, leather lace-up moccasins, and a full feather head-dress. He had painted his chest and face with war paint and held a long spear in one hand and a tomahawk in the other. If Ray stood stationary, he looked like a carved cigar store Indian.

A car approached and made the sweeping turn toward the entrance. Ray took an aggressive step toward the car, stepping out and pushed his spear to the ground in front of the bumper.

The driver slammed on the brakes, skidding to a stop.

Ray approached the car, bent over and stared into the window and gave a loud "whoop," shaking his feathered spear in the air.

The car reversed and squealed backward, almost ending up in the ditch on the other side of the highway. The driver accelerated but then abruptly stopped next to the sheriff's SUV and rolled down his window.

Ray dug his spear into the ground, crossed his arms, resuming his pose. He watched the sheriff, still sitting in his SUV, elbow resting on the open window and chewing on a toothpick, talk to the elderly couple. The old man was flailing his arms with exaggerated gestures and pointing toward Ray.

The sheriff finally got out of the SUV, brushed the wrinkles out of his chinos, adjusted his hat, bent over and gave some directions to the old couple, and moseyed across the road toward Ray.

Ray moved back about twenty feet and was now standing inside the arching sign, the boundary of the reservation.

"Howdy, Ray. You waitin' for the calvary or something?" Sheriff Minor leaned against the sign pole, pulled the toothpick out of his mouth, inspected it, and flicked it into the ditch. "I was eatin' my breakfast and somebody from the casino called and said you was harrassin' their customers."

"Chicken Hawk on reservation land. White man badge no good."

"Cut the crap, Ray. Just tell me what's goin' on so I can get back to my breakfast."

Ray looked up at the sun. "Too late for breakfast."

"You can say that again."

"Too late for breakfast." Ray smiled.

"Aw jeez, Ray, come on, I'll buy you a beer or something. You can tell me all about how the white man persecuted your ancestors or whatever. We just need to let those old folks go in there and lose their money. Hell, *you* get part of it. You should be holdin' their hand and kissin' up to the customers, instead of scarin' the crap out of 'em. Although, the way Martha was talkin'," Miner tilted his head toward the old folks parked up the road, "you better hope she don't get behind the wheel. Somethin' about runnin' over your butt."

Ray straightened up and lost the smile. "Casino build windmills on sacred burial mound. My ancestors spirit cries out. White man sticks it to 'em again. Chicken Hawk tired of carrying around a jar of Vaseline."

"Say what? What burial mound? What's this about windmills?"

Ray threw down the spear and tomahawk and walked across the road and got in the passenger side of Minor's SUV.

Minor started to follow but had to hold up as the old folks pulled into the entrance again and stopped. The old man smiled. "Cowboys kick ass again, huh Sheriff?" The old man looked at his wife and they knocked knuckles, and then proceeded under the giant arch toward the casino.

Minor got in the truck, tilted his hat back, put his hands on the steering wheel, and waited. Ray didn't say anything, just stared straight ahead. Minor finally said, "So, what's the deal? You want me to drive you home, or do you want to go have that beer and talk about this?"

"Drive around back of casino. Chicken Hawk show you white man's blow job."

As Minor put the truck into gear he said, "Cut the Indian talk, okay, Ray. It makes you sound like some kind of moron. I've known you long enough that you don't have to play that game with me." Minor blew out a breath in exasperation. "Okay, let's go look at the mound."

Sitting in the same spot as Ray and Nub had previously, they watched as the work crew toiled with the third stanchion, all neatly positioned in a row atop the mounded earth. Neither said anything, both contemplating the scene.

Ray noticed in the rearview mirror, someone approaching from behind.

The man gave a fake smile to Ray, looking in the passenger window, then looked past him and said, "A little out of your jurisdiction, aren't you Sheriff?"

Minor looked at him with a smirk. "This here's the casino's head of security, Ray. Ain't that right Frank? We are just takin' a look at your, what'd you call it, Ray, a blow job? "

"That's fine, Sheriff, you can watch all you want, even go in and win a thousand or two if you're lucky. But first, if you'll just let Ray out of the cruiser so I can take him into custody for disorderly conduct and harassment on the reservation. He'll be sent before the tribunal and —"

"Hold on there, cowboy," Minor said, "who said anything about arrest? If there's gonna be any arrestin' around here, I'll be the one doin' it. Just stay where you are, Ray."

"May I remind you again, Sheriff, you are now on the reservation and you have no authority. This is sovereign territory. The Tribe Council is the law enforcement agency and they have made me head of security."

"That's *their* problem," Minor snapped. "They want to make some wanna-be gangster head of their security, it don't matter to me. But let me give you some advice. This is *my* county and the reservation is in *my* county. Maybe the feds say I can't exercise any authority on the reservation, but friend, you can't get here without driving on my roads, and if I want to set up a road block at your front entrance and check every loser comin' and goin' for alcohol on their breath, I'll do'er, buddy. So, I'd suggest you don't piss me off any more than I am right now."

Ray continued to stare straight ahead.

Frank took a step back, red faced, his eye starting to twitch.

Sheriff Minor put the car in reverse and backed away from Frank. "Let's go, Ray."

As Minor threw the truck in drive, Ray finally turned his head toward Frank, stuck his arm out the window, showing a stiff middle finger, and said, "*Adios, kimosabe.*"

CHAPTER 13

Lou Luchini sat at the restaurant table, covered with fine white linen and sparkling crystal, leaning back with his hands folded across his stomach, watching his guest swirl deep red wine in the bottom of the large goblet. The guest sniffed the aroma of the '87 French Cab, listed at three hundred and twenty-seven dollars a bottle on the restaurant wine list, while the wine master stood patiently next to the table, ready for the instruction to pour.

"The aroma is so pleasing. That first hint of fruit, but then the bursting scent of tannin, the sign of a truly deep cabernet. And the berries, oh the berries, I can smell the berries. Pour, please pour," Chaganbhai Katton said.

Lou tried to keep the fake smile. What a little mutton-eating weasel. This better be worth it… Ordering three hundred dollar wine. Lou wanted to shove that bottle so far up his ass, he'd smell berries all right. "How does it taste?" Lou forced another smile and shoved his half-eaten cigar in his mouth and chomped so hard he bit his tongue.

His guest, assistant secretary to the state attorney general in charge of state lottery and gaming, had summoned Lou to a meeting regarding certain business dealings involving the casino. After a brief ceremonial meet in Lou's office in the Willis Building, it was suggested they retire to the restaurant located on one of the upper floors near the observation deck.

Katton ordered twin lobster tails as an entre', served with cold smoked Scottish salmon salad. Lou frowned so deeply when the waiter asked about appetizers it caused his face to twitch and his triple chin to turn crimson. Katton decided to pass up that option.

Lou ordered a hamburger, rare, and a diet Coke.

While Katton swirled his wine some more, Lou took the opportunity to address the point of the meeting. "Mister Katton, I'm not quite sure why you are concerned about my leasing arrangement with the casino."

"Please, call me Charles."

"Okay *Charles.*" Lou tried to calm himself. "How's the wine?"

"Oh, it is superb. The flavors are so well melded, and then the tannin lets you know that cabernet is the king of grapes."

And a price fit for a king. "Great, glad you like it. Now, all this concern about my leasing company, I don't understand what it's all about. It doesn't have anything to do with the gaming commission. And the casino is outside your jurisdiction because it's sovereign Indian, so what's your beef?"

"Oh, we have no beef, no beef." Katton looked up from his wine and smiled. "The attorney general merely wants to send his congratulations about your efforts to go green, installing the wind turbines and such. And he wanted to let you know that he and the governor worked very hard to expedite the tax credit your company received. There were many questions regarding, shall we say, the legitimacy of the transaction."

Bingo. He wasn't here for any reason other than to send a message; it was just a shakedown for a donation. They wanted part of the two mil. "So, let me get this straight, as far as the attorney general goes, we're square, and you are just here to enjoy my company and drink a three hundred dollar bottle of wine… on my tab."

"And to thank you for your future support. It's what government's all about, you know, to help assist you and grow your business." Katton watched as the waiter placed his manicured plate of lobster in front of him and offered to pour more wine.

Lou pulled the cigar from his mouth and looked at the gnawed end in contemplation. "I'll tell you what, Charrrrles, why don't you go back and tell the AG, and the governor for that matter, the next time I need their help, I'll call. Okay?" Lou pushed himself away from the table. "And as for that future support you mentioned, I'll send them a copy of your lunch tab marked paid. How's that sound?"

Katton choked up a chunk of lobster and watched Lou's back as he walked out of the restaurant.

♦ ♦ ♦

Lou slammed the door as he came through the reception area headed for his private office suite. The receptionist yelled at his back, "Mister Frank is on the phone from the casino."

Lou shoved a fresh cigar in his mouth and picked up the phone. "Yeah."

"Uh, this is Frank Salucci. I'm at the casino."

"So, that's your job. What you want?"

Frank hesitated. "Maybe this isn't a good time."

"No, it ain't a good time. I've got some muttonhead politician trying to shake me down. I've got the Bureau of Indian Affairs saying I'm desecrating some pile of dinosaur bones. I've got a building full of slot machines with no customers and now I've got you telling me this may not be a good time. If you are that freeking smart, knowin' in advance it might not be a good time, why'd you call?"

"I just wanted to give you a heads up, you know that Indian that wanted to sell us the windmills, the one you had me take a look at?"

"What about him?"

"He's been loitering out in front of the casino, stopping customers and heckling them about the burial mound and the wind turbines."

"So what, I got to do all the thinkin' around here? Call the cops. Get him out'a there."

"I did, but he's friendly with the sheriff, so they didn't do anything."

"Wait a minute, this guy named light something? Wait a minute." Lou shuffled some papers and found the letter from the Bureau. "The Bureau of Indian Affairs sent this letter that I got thirty days to respond. Let's see, da, da, da, must respond to complaint from, da, da, da, here it is, complainant, Raymond Lightfeather. That the guy?"

"Yeah, that's the guy. He dresses up like some movie Indian, carries a spear, the whole nine yards, then stands out near the road and harasses people. I tried to bring him up to the council, but the sheriff wouldn't give me custody, said he would set up alcohol-check roadblocks out in front of the casino if I didn't lay off."

"That's what we get for building a casino out in the middle of nowhere next to some hick town." Lou leaned back in his chair. "Well, we got to do something about this before it gets out of hand. Got any ideas?"

"I suppose I could go find him and teach him a lesson, make him an offer he can't refuse, so to speak."

Lou chuckled. "This ain't New Jersey, you know, although, after that shake-down today, it's hard to tell the difference. No, we don't need that kind of trouble, not yet. He's no different than any of the others, just looking for a handout. Figures if he's a big enough pain in the ass, we'll cough up some dough. I guess it worked. Find him and see what it's gonna take to get him to call the feds and pull this complaint. He'll have to tell 'em it was all a mistake. You wave a grand in his face, that ought'a do it. You still got that bag full of money, don't you?"

He hesitated and said, "Yeah, I suppose I could show him some cash."

"Let me know when I can throw this letter away." Lou hung up.

Chapter 14

"**W**hat is that Indian, featherhead or featherweight, doing with Nub?" Wanda Letterman asked as she looked out the kitchen window over the sink. Ray held the ladder as Nub worked to position a large fin on the back of the fan rotor at the top of the windmill.

Roger sat at the kitchen table munching on a sausage sandwich. Between bites he responded, "It's Lightfeather, Ray Lightfeather. I've told you that a hundred times. I don't know, Nub kind of took a likin' to him and, well, I think it's good for both of them. Ray's a little different, I know, but he's got a lot of common sense. He knows about common things, stuff like, you know, Indian stuff; livin' in the woods, growin' herbs, stuff like that. It's things Nub would never learn in school or on that *computer*."

"You sure he ain't, you know, goofy or something?"

"I've know'd Ray all my life. He's about as good as it gets, once you know him. Now I ain't sayin' Ray's lived a spartan life, somethin' a preacher would be proud of, but he'd give you his last pair of boots if you asked." Roger inspected the end of his sandwich and shoved it in his mouth. "That was good, mom, what'd you put on it?"

"A little bacon grease mixed with sugar and vinegar." Wanda continued to stare out the window. "You think Nub will get that contraption working?"

"I'd bet my last dime on it. One thing for sure, he ain't a quitter. I just hope he don't have to give away no more pigs." Roger pushed back from the table. "I've got to go to the hardware, you need anything from town?"

Wanda grabbed the side of the sink and strained toward the window. "Oh my God, he's gonna fall." She threw herself toward the kitchen door with Roger chasing after her.

Both standing on the porch in aw, they saw Ray catch Nub in mid-air at the bottom of the ladder. The wrench Nub had been using bounced off Ray's shoulder, causing him to jerk, but he held his balance and gently put Nub down feet first and gave him a brush on the head with his hand.

Wanda ran to Nub and hugged him. "Are you all right?... Now, damn it," tears ran down her face, "I told you, Dad, I do not want him up on that ladder like that."

Roger looked at her, then Ray. "You never told me nothin' like that."

"Well, I'm a tellin' you now. Mister featherhead, thank you, if you hadn't been here," Wanda sobbed, "well, I don't know what. Thank you."

"It's Lightfeather Mom," Roger said.

Nub went over and picked up the wrench and headed for the ladder.

Wanda erupted, "Nub, you will *not* get back on that ladder! Are you listening to me?"

"What say we all go to town so Mom can calm down." Roger gave Ray a wink. "Come on, Nub, I got to go to the hardware store, you and Ray can ride along."

◆ ◆ ◆

Over the past few months, Harold Hanover had suffered greatly from the great Hinkley windmill scam. Business at the store was off over fifty percent, his hearing aid had gone on the fritz, Edna had threatened to leave him, probably the only bright spot in his life, and the bank was reneging on his line of credit, preventing him from ordering snow blowers and other winter accessories for the coming season. He sat at his desk staring at the pile of unpaid bills in the basket on the right, and the empty order basket on the left.

His stomach gurgled and he belched. He had eaten so many heartburn remedies lately that he was afraid any further attempts to extinguish the fire were useless.

The front door finally tinkled. Some conversation, even with a non-buyer, was better than dwelling on his problems.

Roger and Nub wandered through the aisle near the grease and lubricants.

Harold came around the counter and leaned against a shelf. "Howdy, Roger. How you doin' today, Nub? Still working on that windmill?"

Roger looked up from the stack of lube tubes and replied, "He's about got it licked. Still has to get the whirly-gig thing up there, but it's startin' to look like it might work."

Harold had a funny sensation, scratched the back of his head, thinking it might be a fly and turned around to find Ray standing uncomfortably close. "Damn, Ray, where'd you come from?"

"Ain't it something, how he does that," Roger said. "'Bout scares the pants off me with his stupid Indian tricks." Roger laughed and Ray smiled, his gold incisor gleaming.

"Ray, you seen the wind-turbines out at the casino?" Harold asked. "Big suckers, somewhere's near sixty or seventy feet tall, I recon."

Ray lost his smile. "Build tur-bines on sacred burial ground. Spirits not happy. There will be trouble, big trouble."

Roger leaned against the shelf. "Ray's not happy about the whole thing, where they put 'em. Built 'em on the burial mound behind the casino. When we was kids, used to find all kinds of arrowheads and artifacts around there. Never knew it was some kind of cemetery though. Just thought it was part of the Olatagwa village."

"Why'd the Indian council let them do that?" Harold asked.

Roger and Harold both looked at Ray.

"Because council not Indian, they are yes men, paid big money by the Las Vegas crooks to bend over and—" Ray looked at Nub. "They take money and look other way."

Nub finally joined the conversation after setting aside a schematic of a string trimmer he had been studying. "It ain't right, building something like that on top of a cemetery where Ray's relatives are buried. What if they built something like that where Grandma's buried? It wouldn't be right."

"They couldn't do that," Roger said.

"So, they can do it at the casino because it's just Indians?" Nub said, crossing his arms.

"That's not what I meant," Roger said. "I mean, it's not the same." Roger looked sheepishly at Ray. "I mean, there's no grave stones on the mound, you know, like a real cemetery, Nub." Roger faked a cough. "Harold, how much is this here lube?"

"It still don't seem right," Nub repeated.

Chapter 15

Frank Salucci called Ray, intending to set up another meeting and lay down the law regarding the incident at the casino. He called numerous times but Ray never answered. On one occasion, someone answered but didn't speak. All Frank said was, "Lightfeather, that you? You better answer the phone. I'm getting sick of this. Your butt's gonna be in a sling if you don't answer. I can only take so much." The phone went dead. Frank even tried using a different phone that would not signal the caller on the receiving end, but Ray still did not answer. He was faced with a decision—which place to stake out, the trailer or the barn. The third choice was the diner, but that seemed above and beyond the call of duty.

The idea of giving Ray a grand just to walk away did not sit well with Frank either, mostly because it was his grand. Even though it had come as a gift, it was still his gift. He decided early in the planning process to use intimidation in lieu of money. It had always worked before and there was no reason to change his routine at this point in the game. Anyway, the money could always be used as a last resort.

Frank spent three hours parked several trailers down from Ray's place, waiting. Two teenagers tried to sell him some pot. One resident came out and inquired about his reason for loitering and tried to bum a cigarette. The park manager, a woman who looked sixty but was probably forty, weighing well past the two hundred mark and smoking a thin cigar, came waddling down the street and asked if he was a cop. When he said he wasn't, she advised they didn't allow no bill collectors or solicitors in the park. Frank told her if she didn't want him there she ought to call a cop. She responded she didn't want no cops here neither, and left.

He gave up the surveillance and headed for the barn.

The morning sun was obscured by dark overcast. Nothing had changed, the muddy path to the barn still showed some use. He was ill prepared again, wearing another pair of loafers.

Ray's truck was nowhere is sight, although there were fresh tracks, so one could assume he may be parked inside the big sliding door. Frank did bring a duffle bag with some accessories, including jaws capable of cutting through a padlock, some basic burglary tools, and a sawed-off shotgun with a pistol grip.

Frank parked a short distance past the old house, retrieved the duffle from the trunk, and carefully picked his way back to the barn, staying on the weeds and ground cover as much as possible to keep his feet dry. Only one window faced the road, it being next to a small door. Next to it was the large sliding barn door. Frank cupped his hands and tried to see inside, but the dirty window and the dark interior gave no hint of the contents. The single door had a hasp and padlock. He made one more cursory survey of the terrain around the barn, making sure no one was watching, and then cut the lock. Before entering, he drew his small .38 and held it at his side, just in case.

He stepped over the threshold and felt the cool air of the interior space along with the musty scent of moldy hay. He knelt down and held the gun out, letting his eyes adjust, fearing there might be some kind of livestock, like a huge bull or a billy goat. Or maybe the crazy Indian had some wild animals as pets. He tried to take in the general lay of the barn. It had room for Ray's pickup inside the door, but the space was empty. Along the wall beyond the big door he found shelving with numerous books and piles of magazines. A desk was positioned near another small window with a kerosene lamp. Another lamp hung from a beam back further in the barn. Old stalls littered with garbage bags outlined the back wall with a half loft overhead loaded with old furniture and other junk.

Frank stepped over to the desk, shuffling papers, trying to draw a picture from the mess of what Ray was up to. If he found bomb-making instruction manuals, he would have some feel for what he was up against. If he found porno, which is what he suspected, it would just contribute to his suspicion that Ray was just another low life.

The desk was cluttered with catalogues and magazines, none of which offered much insight. He did note the *National Geographic* with a picture of a windmill on the front. He pulled out the desk drawers and only found old bills and cancelled checks. In one drawer he found a box of 222 rifle shells. He looked around as far as he could see but found no rifle, just a few boxes stuffed with Indian souvenirs one would find in tourist shops; a couple fake totem poles; some Indian head-dresses, still packed in plastic; a bunch of unopened boxes. Mostly junk.

The wind blew, signaling an approaching storm and the barn groaned under the stress. Frank had an eerie feeling but shook it off; after all, he was still holding the .38. He took methodical steps, scattering straw under his feet, raising the gun while scanning the barn's perimeter, trying to get a better look at the loft. A labyrinth of rope was suspended from an overhead beam and as he drew closer to the middle of the big room, he could see the loft was full of more boxes with some straw bales against one wall.

A whipping rope whirled from above and he instinctively raised the gun. A snare snatched his feet out from under him. His shoulder hit the floor and he was dragged with such force he dropped the gun. Trying to grab at anything and gasping for breath, he tried to gather his senses. He found himself hanging upside down, feet lassoed in the air. Change fell out of his pockets onto the barn floor. He swung like a pendulum, the rope creaking as it scraped the overhead hewn beam. His arms, when outstretched were inches off the floor. The blood pushing against his brain nauseated him.

He tried to pull his torso up to grab the rope around his feet, without success. He grabbed at nothing, helpless, hanging upside down, knowing he would soon end up dead if he didn't get help.

Someone would come. Yeah, Ray would come. Someone would see my car. Surly, someone would come.

From back in the corner of the barn, a high-pitched voice said, "Now whose butt is in a sling?"

Frank twisted, causing his body to slowly turn, hanging from the rope.

Ray walked out of the shadow over to his desk, rested a leg on the corner, and crossed his arms. Silence.

The rope continued to creak as Frank swung. "Okay, you've made your point, Indian boy, now cut me down."

Ray did not speak.

"All right, what's it gonna take? You know, this is considered a felony in most states. I can have you arrested. Even your friend the sheriff won't go along with this."

Silence.

"All right, I'm tired of being mister nice guy. You know, my whole purpose for coming and trying to find you was to give you some money, a gift from the casino. But now you've pissed me off. I mean you've really pissed me off."

Ray rose and took slow strides toward Frank.

"That's better, Let me down and we can sit down and talk this out."

Ray picked up a stick and went to the .38 lying on the floor, picking up the gun without touching it. He walked to the door of the barn, opened it, and flipped the gun out into the mud. He closed the door and walked back to the desk. "Chicken Hawk don't like guns."

The duffle sat next to the desk. Ray opened it and pulled out the shotgun. He broke the barrel and unloaded the single shell. He looked at Frank hanging upside down and still swaying. "You expecting trouble?" Ray sat down at the desk, examining the shotgun, then set it aside and started leafing through a magazine.

"Uh, *Ray*…" Frank said with some frustration, "I'm starting to get a headache here. Cut me down so we can get on with this. I've got some ideas on how we can put all this behind us and everyone will be happy. Now, just let me down before I pass out."

Ray continued to leisurely leaf through the magazine. He got up, picked up the shotgun, took the box of shells out of the duffle, and walked out of the barn.

"Hey, you stupid Indian!" Frank yelled at Ray's back. "Damn it, get back here and cut me down. I swear, I'll—" A blast from the shotgun made the barn shudder. Then another. Then another. The shots rang out for more than a minute. He waited but Ray did not appear. The sound of a truck engine starting sent a shock wave of fear down Frank's spine. Ray was leaving without cutting him down.

Snap, the rope let loose. Frank hit the dirt floor, smashing his shoulder and neck as he tumbled, the rope piling on top of him. The truck rumbled past the barn and down the drive. He tried to stand, dazed and dizzy from the fall. Eventually gaining his feet and throwing the rope aside, he staggered to the door. In the distance, parked along the road, he could see his car, ravaged by the shotgun pellets.

Frank limped to his car. Every window was blown out, the dashboard had a large blast hole, and the front and rear lights were now just bits of broken glass. Frank's face twitched so badly he could hardly see straight. He searched for a stick or log to throw at the already ravaged car. He stomped around, kicked the car door, nearly breaking a toe, and then backed up trying to calm himself. He pulled the car key out of his pocket and gingerly opened the car door, avoiding the broken glass that continued to dislodge from the window frame. He reached in, turned the key and the car started, a relief given the large hole in the dashboard control panel.

Twenty minutes later, Frank limped the car into the parking lot of the Hinkley County courthouse and parked in the sheriff-only parking space next to Sheriff Minor's SUV. He slammed the car door as he got out, spraying broken glass on the parking lot and headed for the sheriff's office entrance with a determined limp.

Sheriff Minor stepped out of the rear door of the courthouse, placed his Stetson on his head, and met Frank limping up the sidewalk. "Well, if it ain't the head Indian himself. A little out of your jurisdiction, aren't you, chief?"

Frank's brain synapses sparked so hot that he saw blue stars swirling around the sheriff. His fists were balled and he feared he might be frothing at the mouth. He opened his mouth but words would not form. Straining, all he could say was, "That fucking Indian. That, that, that fucking Indian..."

Minor leaned against a gatepost, pulled his hat off and brushed it with his shirt sleeve. "And what Indian would we be referring to in such a distasteful tone? Would we be referring to Ray Lightfeather? He doing war chants at the casino again?"

Frank turned and walked back toward the parking lot.

The sheriff followed, getting his hat adjusted on his head. "This your car, Frank? Somebody's gonna have to clean this mess up. You want me to go get you a broom?"

Frank was shaking so bad he placed his palms flat on the hood of his car. "Thaaaat Indian... That Indian shot up my car." Frank got the sentence out but had to gasp for air, trying to keep from hyperventilating. "He also hung me up in his barn. It's kidnapping, attempted murder, felonious assault with a weapon and... and—"

"Hold on there, chief, what in the he-ell are you talking about. You talkin' about Ray, Ray Lightfeather? He did what?" Minor now took the time to walk around Frank's car. "Somebody sure did a job on this car. What'd they use, looks like a shotgun." He leaned in one of the windows and smiled. "Surprised it still runs." Minor stood back up and stretched. "Well, I'm headed for lunch, anything else I can do for you?"

The starbursts in Frank's brain went off like the fourth of July. "You listen to me, you tin-horned bag of wind. I want Ray Lightfeather arrested, and I don't mean tomorrow or tonight, I mean right now. You get on that radio and put out an all-points for his truck, because if you don't, and I find him first, there's going to be one dead Indian, you understand?"

Minor rubbed his protruding chin and studied Frank. "Okay, let me get this straight, chief. You're admittin' right here in front of me that you are gonna leave here and go murder Ray Lightfeather, that right? And as for your car here, how do I know this didn't happen on the reservation, some upset loser gambler decided to get even? Out of my jurisdiction, you know what I mean? So, let me give you a little lesson in how we do things around here, off the reservation, where I have jurisdiction. You listening, *chief*? You want to file a complaint about your car being vandalized, you march right into the office there and Marge will file the complaint. Then, when we have time, we'll go talk to Ray and get his side of the story. In the meantime, given your current state of mind, and the fact you have voiced threats against the life of one of our fine citizens, I would suggest you make yourself scarce, and don't let me find you carrying a gun... off the reservation of course. We understand each other, chief? And, before you leave, clean up this mess." Minor walked around his SUV and before getting in, took one more look at the car, smiled, and shook his head saying, "Man you shore got yourself in a heap of trouble. Yeah, you shore enough did."

CHAPTER 16

Lou sat at his desk with no-neck Rondelo across from him lounging on the couch. He was reviewing some employee complaints gathered from the complaint box in the casino employee lounge. Rondelo maneuvered a quarter up and down the knuckles on his hand with monotonous accuracy.

Lou said, pulling the half-eaten cigar from his mouth, "Listen to this, Joe. This must be one of the waitresses that serve the high-limit slots. She says we ought to put signs on every slot machine saying that the guests are not allowed to touch the servers." Lou looked up at Joe, smiling. "She walks around with all that skin showing and she expects some guy knockin' two hundred dollars a pull down a rat hole not to cop a feel."

Joe took another sip of his cocktail. "Nobody every said they's needed to be smart, just need big knockers and be able to carry a tray."

"Here's another one. 'Please tell whomever left something dead in the employee locker room, locker number twenty-four to get rid of it.'" Lou looked at Joe. "Who puts something like that in the complaint box? Don't we have a janitor over there?"

"Fired him last week, the one that's supposed to do the maintenance and clean the employee lounge and locker room. He's some relative of the Injun that's causing all the problems. Figured they were probably in cahoots so I got rid of 'em." Joe smiled. "I'll get somebody else to check out the locker room. It say what's dead?"

Lou didn't look up from the pile of complaint letters on his desk. "You fire him or have the HR department take care of it?"

Joe lost his smile of confidence. "Well, kind of, I called that babe that handles that stuff and told her to send him a pink slip with his check."

"Since when do you make those decisions? I've told you before, No-neck, you ain't the manager of the casino. We pay Ramón two hundred grand a year to manage the place."

The intercom buzzed and the receptionist said that his eleven o'clock appointment had arrived.

"Joe, you know anything about this, this," Lou shuffled some papers and pulled a pink note from the pile, "this Morning guy? Says he's from the B.I.A."

Joe flipped the quarter in the air and caught it with his other hand. "Never heard of 'em."

Lou cleared his desk by shoving the remaining complaint letters into the wastebasket, saying, "It's Mr. Morning, the guy calls himself mister, this ought to be good. Can't even allow us little people to know his first name. When was the last time the B.I.A. was here anyway? This must have something to do with that Injun's complaint. Okay, let's just listen to him and smile and act like we are sympathetic. You know what that means, no-neck? It means you keep your mouth shut." Lou stuffed the half eaten cigar in his mouth and leaned back in his chair, picked up the phone, and said, "Send him in."

The office door opened and the receptionist allowed a shockingly beautiful woman to enter. Her slim cut business suit covered a silk blouse that billowed open to the cut of the jacket, allowing ample cleavage inspection. The knee-length skirt featured slits up the sides, and the pointed heels accentuated her model-like stature. Her skin tone was dark enough to claim minority status, but with hints of Asian ancestry in her deep-set eyes and straight black hair.

Lou's mouth fell open. The ravaged cigar sagged on his chin. No-neck's whole body turned in the chair, and he too was starry eyed with his mouth hanging open.

Lou pulled the cigar from his lips. "Where's, where's Mr. Morning?"

Mystique looked from one man to the other, adjusting her smile from pleasant to distasteful. "I'm not sure I understand. May I sit down?" Without waiting for an invitation, she moved to the couch and took a seat, laying her briefcase next to her and pulling out a sheaf of papers, crossing her legs and giving a breathtaking view of her thigh.

No-neck's eyes bulged and Lou continued to stare. He finally regained some composure and tried again. "Mary said you were Mr. Morning, I mean, she said Mr. Morning was here. Is he still here, I mean there, or wherever?" He shoved the cigar back in his mouth and chomped.

"As far as I know, there is no Mr. Morning, here, there, or anywhere. My name is Mystique Morning, Assistant to the Undersecretary of the Bureau of Indian Affairs, Midwest region." Her gaze moved from Lou to Joe and back again. "We seem to have a problem and I am here to discuss it, and if necessary, investigate."

Lou smiled. "I didn't know we had no problem. Joe, you know about any problem?"

No-neck continued to stare at the exposed thigh, his mouth open.

Lou asked, "You's seem to be awful young to be, you know, investigatin', or whatever. How'd you get such a big title? Someone must really like you, if you know what I mean." Lou smiled, snagging the cigar from his mouth and throwing one arm over the back of his chair, getting comfortable now and wanting to present his best profile.

Mystique uncrossed her legs and leaned forward. "No one gave me this position, I earned it. I have a degree from Marquette University in Sociology and was appointed by President Obama as Assistant to the Undersecretary. Maybe in your profession, women work their way to the top by getting someone *to like them*, but that's not how it works in my profession."

Lou held up his hands, palms out in retreat. "Sorry, lady. Don't get your undies all bunched up. I didn't mean nothin' like that."

Joe chuckled. "Yeah, nuttin' like that."

Mystique flipped back an errant curl that had fallen across her eye and reached for her file. "We, the bureau, have a complaint from," she glanced at the file, "a Ray Lightfeather, member of the Olatagwa Tribe, complaining about desecration of reservation land." She looked up, making sure she had their attention. "Although Mr. Lightfeather failed to follow protocol, it is still a serious allegation and deserves our attention." She continued, reading from her file, "Our further investigation, after receiving the letter, revealed that the tribe council expanded the footprint of the casino and failed to file an application for Diversion of Property Rights. That would be form number BIA-562390. In addition, there is the application for Restitution and/or Replacement Following Diversion of Property Rights, form number BIA-482762." She looked up from the file and both men stared without expression. "That form was disregarded as well."

Lou pulled the half eaten cigar from his mouth and used it like a pointer aiming at Mystique. "You know, I do remember seeing something about that. You remember that, Joe?" No-neck started to open his mouth but Lou continued, "I think there was a letter about that, the one from the Injun, but I forwarded it to our head of security to investigate. Yeah, that's it, I had him locate Mr. Lightfeather and I think it's all straightened out. It was all a misunderstanding. Now, I'll tell you what, Miss, uh, Miss Morning… kind of has a ring to it, don't it. Why don't we go upstairs and have a nice lunch. Sorry you had to come all the way downtown for nothing, but I'll guarantee you will enjoy the view from the restaurant. Finest wine list in the city."

No-neck rose from his chair, pulled at his pants, checking his zipper, smiled, and said, "I'll get my coat, they's got a dress code, can you believe it?"

"I'm really not interested in dining, Mr. Luchini," Mystique said raising her voice.

No-neck looked at Lou and slowly lowered himself back into the chair.

She continued, "Just what type of conciliatory arrangement did you make with Mr. Lightfeather? Was it monetary? If so, that still does not alleviate the issue of desecration of reservation property."

Lou frowned and put some bite in his tone. "Look, *Miss* Morning, we run a good, clean establishment for the benefit of the Inju… tribe. We send out thousands of dollars every month to the so-called members of the tribe." Lou tilted his head back and forth like a first grader belittling a classmate. "And now one of 'em decides he wants to screw up the whole works for all of 'em. You think that's right, huh? I tol' you, we talked to this guy and he changed his mind. He don't want to complain no more. *Got it*? So why don't you go back to your boss and tell 'em everything's just fine out there on the reservation." He shoved the cigar back in his mouth with vigor and rose from his chair, giving a big smile. "You might even find something for your trouble when you gets home. We try to treat our friends nice, if you knows what I mean."

Mystique eyed Lou and then No-neck's blank stare. She placed the file back in her briefcase, closed it, and rose from the couch. "Thank you for your time."

"So's, the matter's closed. Good. Joe, be sure we take good care of Miss Morning." Lou smiled, holding out his cigar and waving goodbye like a two-year-old.

Mystique moved across the room toward the door like she was walking down the runway at a Paris style show. She turned and said, "No, the matter is not closed, Mr. Luchini. Actually, I would say the scope of the investigation just took on a new look, now including obstruction of justice and attempt to bribe a federal official."

The door closed, leaving nothing but a whiff of Chanel for their enjoyment.

CHAPTER 17

Frank sat in the casino security office fuming from his encounter with the sheriff and Ray. He twitched and felt dizzy from near hyperventilation. When he entered the office, one of the floor security officers walked up behind him and put a hand on his shoulder in a friendly manner and Frank drew down on him with his mud caked .38. Frank's way of letting them know he should be left alone.

He pushed papers and unopened mail around his desk. He had visions of Ray hanging from a totem pole for target practice and of stuffing E-4 plastic explosives under the seat of Sheriff Minor's SUV and smiling when it disintegrated in a ball of fire. He even caught himself talking out loud to no one, blurting out expletives and slamming his fist on the desk in exasperation.

The phone on his desk rang for the fifth time before it broke his fragmented concentration. He grabbed it and yelled, "What do you want?"

There was a lingering silence and then, "Who is this? Is this Frank? Who answers the phone like that? This is Luchini, who is this?"

Frank exhaled and rubbed his forehead. "Yeah, it's Frank. Sorry, I'm just a little upset here."

"About what?"

Frank looked at his balled fist and the dirt smudges on his shirtsleeve and debated whether to enter into an explanation of how his day had gone so far. He could hear Lou breathing into the phone, waiting. "I had a little run in with the Indian, the one causing the problems down here. And then I had a meeting with the local sheriff and that ended up being a waste of my time."

"I thought you were going to get everything straightened out with the Indian. I thought we had that all settled. You offer him something to go away, like we discussed?"

Frank's hand that held the receiver was going into a spasm and sparks twinkled in front of his eyes. He opened his mouth but found it difficult to speak through gritted teeth. "I, I, I'm still working on it."

"You want I have to send No-neck down there to straighten this out? What gives, you go puss on me, Frank? I got some babe from the BIA breathing down my neck, threatening to open an investigation and you tell me you are still *working* on it?"

Frank's eye was twitching so bad he took his free hand and covered it. "I tol' you I am working on it. As soon as I find the Indian, he won't be a problem no more, to nobody."

The line was quiet for a minute, then Lou said, "Just take care of it and don't make me have to call no more." The line went dead.

♦   ♦   ♦

Frank spent the next day provisioning for the task at hand. From his storage unit, he retrieved a camo jump suit, camo jungle hat, and infantry boots. He stuffed his backpack with essentials, knowing his recon of the barn could be a lengthy proposition. To complete his ensemble, he shouldered a Remington 700-308 with a mil-dot tactical ten by fifty scope.

Prior to driving to Ray's property, he studied a typographical map of the township section, orienting the best path into the target area. His plan entailed parking about a mile away on an adjacent township road and trekking cross-country to a vantage point behind the barn, setting up, and waiting. Once he made visual contact with Ray, the plan got a little frayed. He envisioned hanging Ray feet first from the barn beam, giving him a view out of the big barn door while he destroyed his truck with a baseball bat. Maybe tying him to one of the fake totem poles in the yard and letting him watch while the barn burned with the truck inside. Of course, he could just shoot Ray from a half mile away, but that seemed too polite. There were just so many options, each bringing a smile as he prepared for the stakeout.

He parked down a lane next to a pasture, a quarter mile from a ramshackle farmhouse. An old man sat on the porch and never moved as Frank climbed a fence and started across the expanse of long grass. Halfway across the open field, he noticed a large bull eyeing him from a swale crest overlooking a small pond. The farther Frank moved toward the wooded end of the pasture, the closer the bull came, trotting a few yards, stopping, and then trotting a few more yards, closing the gap.

Frank stopped, picked up a rock, and threw it in the direction of the animal. The bull looked at the rock rolling by and then back at Frank with what appeared to be a slobbery smile.

The slobbery smile produced a loud grunt. The bull charged, throwing clods of dirt up in his wake. Frank ran for the tree line. The rifle slid off his shoulder and the muzzle drove into the mud. He dove over the fence, landing in a briar patch full of thorns. The rifle barrel was buried in the mud and the scope, after glancing off a limb, snapped off at the mounting.

Gathering the broken gun and disengaging from the thorn bush, Frank rubbed the blood from the scratches on his face, took one last look at the bull, and pushed on through the woods. His woodsman skills were sorely lacking even though he carried a hand-held compass. After a half hour walk following a ridgeline he assumed would take him to Ray's barn, he arrived at the same pasture fence where he started, the bull looking up while lounging near the pond and wearing the same slobbery smile.

Frank gave a disgusted sigh. How long would it be before the blister on his foot inside the stiff leather boot would fester? He turned and headed back into the woods. This time he concentrated on walking in a straight line and watching the compass. He came upon a small creek riffling through a cut in the woods. The water was muddy from recent rain but it didn't look deep. He took an initial step into the water and found the footing firm and only a few inches deep, so he took another step. The creek bed dropped off and Frank fell face first into the water, struggling to gain footing and hold onto his gun and pack. He finally grabbed a bush sticking out from the opposite bank and pulled himself onto the rocks and sand. His boots filled with water. Completely soaked, he crawled into the vines and tall grasses and lay there with his eyes closed, gasping for breath. He shivered, the unpleasant thought of continuing his trek in this condition impeding any motivation to stand up.

Frank finally opened one eye, looked up through the canopy of the low-hanging branches into the sky, sighed, sat up, and leaned against a vine-covered tree. Standing on the other side of the stream looking at him was Ray, dressed in jeans, his leather vest, and a red bandanna around his head. He held a thick walking stick and stood silent, a wry smile across his rugged countenance.

Frank pulled up the broken gun and pushed the bolt action, advancing a cartridge into the breach, causing water to squirt and mud to fly. Having a bead on Ray, he smiled and said, "Nice seeing you, Ray. Taking a little walk in the woods today?" Frank lost his smile. "I wouldn't plan on making it home."

Ray just stared at Frank without comment.

"A little less talkative when I'm holding the gun, huh, Ray?"

Ray smiled again. "Poison ivy. White boy sitting in poison ivy."

Frank looked around. He didn't know what poison ivy looked like so he had no idea if Ray was just trying to divert his attention. "So what? I guess it's better than laying in the mud with a slug in my forehead, like you're gonna be."

Ray knelt down, pulling a long grass stem from the stream bank and put it in his mouth. "Muzzle full of mud. Gun blow up in face."

Frank's hands started to spasm, sparks swirled around Ray's face. His blood pressure was peaking and he raised the rifle to his shoulder. Then he thought back to the episode at the fence and the muzzle of the gun burying in the mud. He remembered his military basic training and the sergeant's admonition that a blocked muzzle was a sure way to loose both eyes when the gun backfired. But he couldn't back down. "You think I'm going to fall for that crap? You think I'm so stupid I'll just let you walk away?"

Ray stood up. "All white men stupid, some just worse than others." Ray turned and walked back into the trees.

Frank's finger shook against the trigger as he looked down the barrel at Ray's back. In disgust, he threw the rifle into the weeds and pulled at his backpack, trying to find his pistol, but by the time he pulled it out, Ray had disappeared into the woods.

No use chasing the Indian in his current condition. He looked around, *poison ivy?*

◆   ◆   ◆

Frank awoke restless, clawing at his arms and neck. It was like he had ants crawling all over him. Everything was blurry and he rubbed his eyes trying to focus. He scratched at his arms and then his neck. The attempts just seemed to amplify the irritation. An overpowering thirst led him to the bathroom. Searching for a glass, he looked in the mirror but his focus was marred. All he could see was a big red blob with hair on top and slits for eyes. His face had a rough, puffy feel, like touching a rotten orange. Must be a dream, but there was too much realism. He clawed at the junk clinging to his eyelashes, trying to get a better look.

Poison ivy! He leaned closer to the mirror and rubbed again, seeing his swollen hand and puffy wrist, milky puss oozing from the peppered skin where he had scratched during the night.

That stupid Indian.

CHAPTER 18

Frank walked into the diner after visiting the Hinkley Pharmacy and being advised by the pharmacist, the only over the counter remedy for poison ivy is calamine lotion, unlikely to help in such an extreme case, and that it was best to avoid scratching or making contact with other extremities, especially those between the legs.

Maria came to the end of the counter, stopped a few steps from Frank, and said, "*Que es* that? Man, chew got a *muy grande* rash." Maria came a little closer, tilting her head and inspecting Frank's face. Then she looked over her shoulder in a conspiratorial stance, making sure no one was listening. "Chew want some medicine? I get especial salve from Mexico. It makes rash go away, no matter where it is, chew know what I mean?"

Frank stared at Maria through his only, partially open, swollen eye. The other was clamped shut like an angry clam. "This isn't a rash, you dumb..." Frank sighed. Not much use getting mad a Maria. "It's poison ivy. Can I get a cup of coffee?"

Maria retreated and returned with the coffee pot. She stretched to reach Frank's cup, keeping as far way from him as she could. "Chew really should try my salve."

"You seen Ray? I need to talk to him."

"Hee's stuff don work. I tried it. It yust make it worse."

"What?" Frank said looking up from his coffee.

"Hee's cream, hit don work. I tried it. Then *mi madre* send me the salve from Mexico. Hit cleared right up."

"I don't care about his cream, I just need to find him. You know where he is?" Frank's red, swollen hand was starting to cramp.

"He's popular today, that *senorita* over there es looking for heem too."

A seductive, well-dressed, dark haired woman sat in a booth reviewing some documents. She was so far out of place among the locals that there was almost an aura about her, like a silhouette around the moon on a misty night.

"She tell you what she wanted, why she's looking for Ray?"

Maria turned to serve another customer. "Don know."

Frank shuffled over to the young lady's booth, trying to get a look at the papers she had spread out as he passed.

The lady looked up as Frank passed, showing obvious displeasure at the site of his swollen face by putting her hand on her brow, like she was shielding herself from the sun, and looked back down.

Frank turned and lingered long enough to arouse the lady's suspicion, and then saw her pull a dollar bill from her purse.

"Here, take this and get yourself a cup of coffee, " she said, stretching her arm to distance herself.

Frank looked at the dollar bill and frowned. "What, you think I'm some kind of bum? I already have coffee at the bar, so put it away. I'm wondering why you are looking for Ray Lightfeather."

She couldn't avoid looking at the blotchy red face. "Are you a relative or something? You should see a doctor about that rash."

"Yeah, so I've been told. I'm just a friend. Actually, I do some business with Ray and need to talk to him. You know where he is? He's tough to contact. Never answers his phone."

She responded, "I've noticed that. Tried to call him several times and only get an answering machine. What kind of business is he in that you need to contact him?"

"He sells Indian relics, mostly fake. Lives in a trailer out near the Walmart, but he's never there. So, what's your business, why're you looking for him?" Frank moved a little closer, allowing some patrons to pass by in the aisle.

She moved farther into the booth, away from Frank. "I just need to talk to him, it's personal. I'll let him know you are looking for him, if I see him. I didn't catch your name."

"Sam, uh, Sam Coldwater, Coldwater Investments, nice to meet you." Frank turned, sensing another patron wanting to pass and found Maria standing behind him, holding the pot of coffee.

"Excuse me… *Sam.*" Maria smiled at Frank. She looked at the woman. "Chew want more coffee? Chew ready to order?" Maria took out her pad and slipped between Frank and the booth, leaning over, ready to scribble the order.

Frank, now completely in everyone's way, retreated to the diner counter and sat back down, his frustration boiling over as he clawed at the raw skin on his neck. He watched as the young lady slipped Maria a business card wrapped in a twenty-dollar bill and Maria shoved it under her EZ tatoo.

♦　♦　♦

Ray's phone buzzed for about the twentieth time and it wasn't even ten o'clock. He opened the phone but did not offer a greeting.

"Ray, bambino, chew there? Listen, the real estate guy is here and there is a senorita, she no tell me her name…Ey Chiwawa, chew should see hees face, hees face looks like the cook's chili sauce… Si, I tol' heem to use your cream…Poison ivy? Hit don look like ivy to me, hit's a rash…Si, she gave me a number… I'll tell her. Ray, bambino, I mees chew."

♦　♦　♦

Ray entered Ralphy's bar through the back door, pausing in the shadows to survey the room. He had instructed Maria to arrange an appointment with the woman around noon at the bar, and although there was a healthy lunch crowd, the mystery woman stood out like a Barbie doll in an ogre factory. She sat in a booth against a far wall. Her black hair shimmered in the low light and her long legs garnered stares from every man in the room. Now that he knew what he was dealing with, Ray straightened his vest, tried to rub dust off his boots, and removed his Stetson. He was about twenty minutes late for the pre-arranged meeting and the lady, gathering some papers she had spread on the table, looked like she was preparing to leave.

He crossed the room, approaching her from the back and in one motion swung his large body into the booth across from her. He folded his large hands with elbows on the table and looked into her eyes without comment.

She lifted her coffee cup and took a dainty drink, returned it to the table, and said, "You must be Ray."

Ray still did not respond.

"I'm Mystique Morning, from the BIA, Ray, here to talk to you about your letter of complaint about the Olatagwa casino and the alleged desecration of sacred Indian property." The intro sounded like it came out of a book. She looked down at her coffee and then back up, spellbound by Ray's penetrating dark eyes. "Ray, we take these accusations serious. Do you want to tell me about it?" The mesmerizing stillness of Ray's posture and expression continued to erode her confidence like a snowdrift in the spring.

Ray's dark eyes, the lined dark skin surrounding the high cheek bones and the black hair with hints of gray pulled back into a braid, told an enchanting story without words, like looking at an image of the old west. Ray's hands were still folded in front of him on the table, his leather vest occasionally squeaking against the vinyl seat. He too, found himself mesmerized by Mystique's beauty. Her eyes, dark spots in a sea of white and veiled by long lashes that fluttered when she talked and could also hold a firm stare.

"How you get this job, assistant to somebody?" Ray spoke in a hushed tone.

"I, I don't know how that, I mean, I don't think that has anything to do with your complaint." She felt hot inside, even though her coffee was barely warm. An emotional tremor then gave her a chill. She rubbed her forehead

"It has nothing to do with the complaint. I'm asking about you. You wanted to talk to me, to investigate. I am talking to you, and investigating." Ray smiled.

Mystique relaxed into the cushioned seat, getting comfortable with the conversation and she said, "I was appointed to the position by the President, well, not him personally. I helped during his campaign and, well, you know how that works."

"In the language of the Ancients, it's echew aca adoo baba onie. You scratch my back, I scratch yours."

Mystique straightened and raised an eyebrow. "Wow, I'm *impressed*. You know the native language of your tribe?"

Ray smiled. "No, I just made that up."

Mystique's eyes twinkled and she squinted from the broad smile as she broke out in laughter along with Ray.

Once again she leaned back and folded her hands. "Actually, this is my first venture out into the field, I mean, away from the office. For a while, I was just given assignments no one else would take, like babysitting my bosses Schnauzer while he and his girlfriend went on vacation." She stared at her hands. Then this assignment came up and everyone else was busy— Anyway, we are here to talk about you, and your issue with the casino."

Ray looked down at his folded hands and drew in a breath. "The casino builds windmills on my ancestors' burial ground. It's sacred ground. They think they can buy the silence of my brothers. They cannot buy my silence."

"Have they talked to you? Have they offered you money to stay quiet?"

Their hands inched closer together across the table, like magnets giving in to the invisible force.

Ray smiled again, causing Mystique's face to brighten as well. "They sent someone to, maybe persuade me to change my mind. He ran into some trouble with his car."

"Is his name Sam?"

"Doesn't matter what name he uses, he is easy to see, his head looks like a squashed tomato." Ray smiled again.

"Ah, yes, I think I met him at the diner. He asked me if I knew how to find you. I'm sure he asked E.Z. the waitress too. But then, you probably know that." Mystique leaned back and crossed her arms. "Ray, I really get the feeling that this means a lot to you, not only that, you seem to be enjoying it, and that it's more important than money. We both know the casino spreads a lot of money around, but you don't care, do you?"

"It's white man's money, it's not my money. They steal the land to build a casino so they can steal the money from their own people, then they steal what's left. I don't need their money and it's too late to take revenge for the past, but I can do something about the future. Anyone can be fooled once, but only a fool gets fooled twice."

Mystique leaned in toward Ray. "I suppose you can make up some Indian language for that too."

"If you want."

"No, not necessary. But what do you mean? I mean, I know what it means," Mystique brushed hair away from her face, drawing on the space in time to compose. She blew out a breath and started again, "What do you mean, get fooled *twice*?"

"When they wanted to build the casino, they told the tribe elders everyone would get rich, everyone being anyone with Olatagwa blood. I knew then it was a scam because I can count on my fingers the number of Olatagwa descendents around here. Anyway, they had to get my vote since I am one of the few remaining true blood descendents, and get my name on the petition to start the proceeding for reservation designation. At first I wouldn't do it, but then all of these wanna-be Indians came out of the woodwork and blamed me for keeping them from getting a casino welfare check. Finally, I decided it wasn't worth the hassle and signed on. When they finally got the thing built and running, I find out it's run by a bunch of crooks out of Las Vegas. They send out a bunch of checks every month and all of the bars around here are happy for a few days, but then everything returns to normal until the next check is mailed.

"So, they fooled me once, but never again."

Mistique said, tilting her head, "What about the wind thing, what do you think ought to happen?"

"I'm sure nothing will happen. They already paid off the chief of the tribal council. I'm the only one that cares. I'll make them miserable for a while; keep their goon busy. It's kind of fun." Ray looked around the bar. The lunch crowd was clearing out. "You want to go see the blow job?"

Mystique had her coffee cup near her mouth and about dropped it. "*What?*"

"Go see the job site where they are installing the wind tur-bines. I call it a blow job." They both laughed.

"Sure, we can take my car."

CHAPTER 19

Frank stared into the mirror in the casino employees' locker room with his one open eye, smearing Maria's salve over his swollen face. He had given her one hundred dollars for an un-labeled four-ounce jar of sticky goop that smelled like a mixture of dirty diaper and spoiled milk. She guaranteed that the swollen mass would disappear in one day.

One of the security personnel stuck his head through the door into the locker room and said, "Frank, there's a car out by the loading docks with government plates. Looks like two people but the windows are tinted and the security camera is a little blurred. God, what's that smell? You sick or something?"

"I'll be there in a minute." Frank continued smearing the goop on his face and then moved to his neck and arms until the entire bottle was empty. Where the skin on his face had been beet red with pus blisters when he started, it was now starting to turn into purple splotches, oozing pinkish plasma. He squinted at the mirror. It must be working.

In the security office, he leaned over the video screen showing the loading-dock area. An undercurrent of comments came from the other guards, complaining about the smell permeating the room as everyone moved away from Frank. Ignoring them, he studied the sedan, identifying the government license plate and then switched to another camera view that gave a better look at the profile of the car. The passenger window lowered half way and Frank got a good view of the occupant.

Frank jumped up and looked around the room. "You, you, and you, come with me. Bring your weapon." None made a move as he headed for the door, pulling his .38 from his waistband holster. Frank yelled, "You heard me! Let's go, right *now*."

Frank ran down the hall toward the employee-only elevator with the others in hot pursuit. He barked instructions as they rode to the ground floor. "We will go out through the east loading dock, weapons drawn. Surround the vehicle. If whoever is driving tries to leave, take out the tires."

"But boss, it's a fed car. What if there're F.B.I.? I ain't shooting it out with no fed." The guard waved his hand under his nose, gasping.

"You let me worry about that. Just hold your position. I'll do the talking. The passenger is a fugitive and I'll make the arrest. If he runs, I'll do the shooting." They huddled at the loading-dock door. "Okay, everyone ready? Let's go."

♦ ♦ ♦

All three stanchions were erected and the giant propellers were installed on two, with the third lying on the ground next to a crane. No workmen were present but the project was nearing completion.

Mystique and Ray stared in silence.

"So, they burned the bodies on top of that hill?" Mystique asked.

"Once the spirit has risen from the high point, the remains are returned to the earth."

The clatter of shoes on pavement interrupted the explanation. A guard ran in front of the car with gun drawn. Another guard stood a few feet away from Mystique's door, gun drawn as well.

Frank stuck his gun through the window at Ray's head and said, "Gotcha."

Ray turned to Frank. "That's a nasty rash, Frank. Musta used Maria's salve. I can tell by the smell."

Through gritted teeth Frank ordered, "Get out of the car, *now*. Get down on the ground with your hands behind your back. You make one move I don't like, there's gonna be smart-ass Indian brains all over the inside of this car."

Ray turned to Mystique and smiled. "Remember the squashed tomato face I told you about? That's him."

Mystique said, "Hi, Sam. You shouldn't point guns like that. What seems to be the problem?"

"Shut up… Ray, I'm giving you a three count to get out of the car. One —"

"Sam," Mystique said, "you know who I am?"

"Two —"

"Sam, I'm a federal agent from the Bureau of Indian Affairs. Do you know what that is, Sam?" Mystique bent down to make eye contact with Frank.

"So what? This guy is a fugitive. I'm taking him into custody. You want to watch, that's fine. Once he gets out of the car, you want to leave, that's fine too." Frank looked back at Ray. "What's it gonna be, Ray? You want to resist arrest? I hope you do because it would be a pleasure to take you down." The purple splotches on Frank's face turned into dark mounds of bloody mush. His swollen eye was popping out like that of a desert lizard.

Mystique shook her head in disgust. "Sam, Sam, Sam…You know, right now you are guilty of accosting a federal officer, false arrest, let's see, probably several other felonies involving a gun." She hit the button on her window and looked out at the other guards and said, "By the way, that goes for all of you."

The other guards slowly lowered their guns and holstered them, looking at each other for direction on what to do next.

Mystique's voice raised an octave. "So Sam, you want to back the *hell* off."

Frank didn't move, some goop dripping off his chin.

"So here's the way I see it," Mystique said, "I can call in the calvary, that would be the FBI, BIA unit, and have you all hauled out of here in a prison wagon." The other guards looked at each other again and all started a fast retreat to the loading dock. "Or, I can just make a call and have the whole casino shut down for a month or so until we sort all this out. What's it gonna be," she leaned a little closer, "*Sam?*"

Frank's hand shook and clenched from spasm. He moved the gun away from Ray's head to avoid a deadly accident. The crap Maria had sold him was slowly mixing with the sweat on his face and getting on his lips and into his mouth and causing him to gag. He turned and looked at the backs of the other guards leaving through the overhead door of the loading dock.

Ray noticed the second of inattention by Frank and hit the up button on the window, trapping Frank's hand as it closed.

Frank yelled, "Shit, shit, shit, you're breaking my wrist!"

The gun fell harmlessly into Ray's lap and he said calmly, "Let's go."

Mystique looked at Frank's swollen purple mush of a face, the one good eye staring back in amazement while he struggled to free his hand and said, "What about him?"

"He'll keep up, for a while."

She put the car in gear and started to roll.

Frank yelled, "No! Stop, stop!" He humped along trying to run with his arm being stretched like a dried out rubber band. When he finally started to tumble and Ray knew he was going down, he opened the window and Frank spilled onto the pavement, rolling twice and skidding to a stop against a Buick Century waiting at a cross lane.

An old man with a heavy mustache and thick glasses that looked a lot like Wilfred Brimley, leaned out of his window and looked down a Frank. "Damn boy, you's ought to be more careful. Now get away from my car."

Frank pushed himself up with his swollen hand and started to respond but the old man promptly drove ahead running over Frank's hand with his rear tire.

♦ ♦ ♦

Frank dragged himself to the side entrance of the casino holding his raw, smashed fingers and trudged through the crowd back to his office. He paid no attention to people in his way, pushing with his shoulder, kicking stools as he plowed through the crowd. Some started to push back but the impact of the stench along with his mauled face, stymied their antagonistic enthusiasm.

Reaching the employee locker room, he found some gauze and wrapped his hand. He was shaking so bad he had difficulty completing the procedure. He glanced up into the mirror and was shocked at the condition of his face. Everyplace he had smeared the salve, there seemed to be mounds of purple mush.

Frank returned to his office, lay down on the couch, and stared up at the ceiling through his one open eye.

Stupid Indian.

♦ ♦ ♦

Mystique and Ray drove along in silence for a mile or so, and then looked at each other and started to laugh.

"Did you see his face just before you opened the window? Imagine seeing that look in your window late at night." Mystique had trouble getting the statement out she was laughing so hard.

"I told you it was kind of fun, screwing with the white man." Ray still had the gun in his lap. As they crossed a creek bridge he threw the gun out. They approached a cross road and Ray said, "Turn here, I want to show you something."

Ray directed Mystique down a long lane toward the Letterman farm.

As they approached the house, the windmill came into view, now, at least from appearance, complete.

"This is Roger Letterman's place. He's a hog farmer."

Mystique waved her hand under her nose. "I noticed."

"Depends on which way the wind's blowin'. See the windmill? Nub built that. He's their kid, 'bout eleven, I suspect. But, he's special, I mean, he's got special talent. Smartest kid, or adult I ever met."

Roger Letterman exited the machinery shed wiping his hands with a dirty rag, one strap of his bib overalls hanging down over his bare shoulder.

Ray opened his door and eased his long legs out and leaned against the car, waiting for Roger to approach.

"Scared the pants off me, Ray. I thought you was the FBI or something and was coming after Nub." Roger gave a squint of concern and rubbed the sweat off his forehead again. "What they got you for, Ray?"

Ray just smiled and said, "Nothin' yet."

Mystique stepped out of the car and Ray made the introductions, saying nothing more than Mystique was a friend. "Where's Nub? He home from school yet?" Ray checked his watch.

"In the barn, I suppose. He spends most of his time in there on that damned computer."

The screen door on the barn slammed and Nub walked toward the car, smiling. "Hey, Ray."

Ray once again made the introduction. Nub barely noticed Mystique and talked directly to Ray. "I got it working, Ray. I had to gear it way down to get enough power to turn the generator, but it works. Produces about three hundred watts. Ain't much considering the generator would produce ten thousand if it was hooked up to the diesel." Nub looked up at the blades he had formed out of roof sheet metal. "No wind today. Yesterday, it worked all day. I got it hooked up to that mercury light over the barn door. When the power reaches one hundred watts, a circuit automatically opens and the light comes on." Nub smiled at Ray.

"Like I told you, Missy," Ray said, "this boy is special. Give him time, he'll probably have the whole farm wired to this thing."

"Let's hope not," Roger said, "it already cost me three hogs."

Ray asked Nub, "You want to show Missy your lab?"

"Sure." Nub turned toward the barn, Ray and Mystique following.

Roger gave warning. "Let me know if he has any, you know, pictures he ain't supposed to look at in there."

Nub's so-called lab consisted of a small room with boards suspended between two sawhorses for a desk. His computer and associated equipment were positioned on the boards with piles of magazines and books scattered around. He had drawings nailed to the walls and wires strung everywhere.

"This is pretty impressive," Mystique said. "Do you have a play station or any of the other cool toys?"

"Naw, I mostly just use the computer to access the web and download programs."

"You had a chance to work on that thing we talked about?" Ray asked.

"I think I've got it figured out but I need their IP address," Nub responded, fooling with the computer keyboard.

"That something I get at the post office?"

Nub laughed. "No, it's kinda like their computer address, an address that the mainframe in California uses to connect with the local server to send instructions. You'll need someone over there to get it for ya. I can't get it from here. Once I have that, it's simple."

♦ ♦ ♦

Mystique and Ray rode in silence for a while and then Mystique had to inquire. "What was that stuff about the IP address you asked Nub?"

"Just havin' fun screwing with the white man, that's all."

CHAPTER 20

Harold Hanover opened the last piece of mail on his desk, appearing to be an invitation addressed to the President of the Hinkley County Chamber of Commerce. So far he had opened three bills, a collection letter from one of his suppliers, and a solicitation from a credit-card company that had already turned him down the month before. The invitation had raised gold lettering and read:

> V.I.P. PASS
> *Your presence is requested,*
> *Olatagwa Casino and Convention Center*
> *Friday, October 18*
> *12:30 PM*
> *Ribbon Cutting and Reception*
> Celebrating Initiation of Our
> Ecologically Friendly Alternative
> Energy Project
> *r.s.v.p.*

No reason he should decline, even though the Chamber Board had tried to rescind his appointment as president. An afternoon at the casino being wined and dined by the management was just what he needed.

The store door bell tinkled and Harold stood up to see Red Redderson, Editor of the Hinkley *Messenger* stepping to the back of the store. Harold sat back down.

"Hi, Harold," Redderson said, looking around at the empty store, "business off a little this month?"

Harold sighed. "It could be better, fall's always a little slow." He continued to stare at the paperwork instead of Redderson, knowing what was coming next.

"Haven't got your check for last month's insert. I know you said it was co-op from your supplier, but maybe I could get your half today.

Any chance of that?" Redderson pulled a sucker out of the candy bowl and shoved it in his half smiling mouth.

Harold finally looked up, trying to invent an excuse for buying some more time on his account when he noticed one of the gold-embossed invitations sticking out of Redderson's shirt pocket behind his row of pens. "See you got an invitation too," Harold said, pointing toward Redderson's pocket.

Redderson looked down at the invitation. "Yeah, press pass. It'll be a free lunch and it'll get them a front-page story, free advertisement. They usually put out a nice spread. Did a nice feature last week on the project, you see it?"

"I think I did. Nice story you wrote." Harold had no idea what he was talking about.

"You know, they built those things right on top of the Indian mound. One of the construction guys said when they put the foundation in for the first pole or tower, whatever, they dug up a bunch of bones. Said they figured it was animal bones, deer or something, and then I guess Ray Lightfeather started making a big stink about the stuff being built on the mound and the construction guys put two and two together, but it's too late, already hauled the dirt away." Redderson dug around in the candy dish, putting a couple more suckers in his pocket.

"Anyway," Redderson continued, "I call the casino, you know, doing my reporter duty, trying to get the rest of the story, and they refer me to the Chicago office and I talk to one of the big cheeses, and he tells me the Bureau Of Indian Affairs has been there and cleared the whole project. Tells me they investigated the bone story and it was all a hoax, something Ray Lightfeather put out there to try to stop the project. So, I tried to get a hold of Ray to confirm that part and couldn't ever find him, so I had to drop that part of the story. Had to make the story more a feature about their ecological concern, crap like that. Then I get this invitation and guess what's included in the envelope," Redderson smiled, "three one hundred dollar chips for the casino. You get any of those with your invitation?"

Harold picked up the opened envelope still lying on the desk and shook it. "I guess not," But then, he didn't get used as a shill for their scam.

"If you see Ray, I'd still like to talk to him. He's tough to find. But then, he's an Indian, I guess it's in his genes. You gonna write that check?"

Harold was hoping he had forgotten. "Uh, I'm right in the middle of paying my bills for this month. I'll drop it off or get it in the mail, if I haven't done it already."

"Sure," Redderson said, "the second biggest lie, the check's in the mail."

♦ ♦ ♦

Frank parked behind the Kountry Kitchen and walked through the kitchen and sat down at the end of the counter.

Maria wandered toward him but stopped some distance away, her mouth open in shock. "Frank, *es* that chew? Oh bambino, chew is a mess."

Frank stared through his one open eye, his un-bandaged swollen hand shaking, and said through clenched teeth, "That stuff you sold me, see what it did... *Do you*? I used that whole jar of crap and all it did is make it worse. Give me my hundred back."

Maria looked around, then came a little closer. "Chew yoos the whole jar? Franky bambino, chew yust yoos a leetle bit. Hits *muy* strong. I yust yoos a leetle bit," she held up her finger, "on my finger, and hit clear right up. I tol you, yust a leetle bit."

"You didn't tell me anything. My face looks like I went ten rounds with George Foreman and it ain't getting any better. Give me my hundred bucks and I'll go see a real doctor."

"Chew want some coffee?" Maria turned and walked away.

Frank stared at a picture of President Obama hanging next to some day-old donuts wrapped in cellophane behind the counter and said to no one, "I got to go back to Vegas."

♦ ♦ ♦

"Lance, I need that favor we talked about." Ray sat in his pickup in the Wal-Mart parking lot, watching the entrance to his mobile home park while he talked to Lance Thrustworthy.

"A *favor*?" Lance replied. "You get me fired from a cake job, make me sit at home with your fat aunt, and *you* need a *favor*? Think again, pal."

"Yeah, well, I'm sorry about that, but it wasn't my fault they decided to destroy my ancestors' graves. You should be as upset as me."

"Why? I'm Irish, and now I'm unemployed. That's the only thing I'm upset about."

This was not going in the right direction. "Look, all I'm askin' is to get that information for me. When it's all over, you'll have a good laugh." Ray could hear his aunt in the background barking out some complaint about mud on the floor.

Lance yelled away from the phone, "Stuff a sock in it!" Then he said to Ray, "What I get for marrying a damn squaw. See Ray, what I think is funny and what you think is funny, it's two different things. You think standing out in the middle of the highway in your shorts with a spear in your hand is funny. I think Jay Leno is funny, two different things. So, don't tell me I'll be laughing when you get done with whatever you got planned. Now, afterwards, if they cart you away in a cruiser with the lights flashing, that would be funny."

"So, you won't help me?"

"You been listening to me, Ray? You deaf or just stupid?" Lance sighed. "I'll tell you what, Ray, you get my job back — I mean the *same* job, and I'll help you, as long as it don't involve killin' nobody. I'll get that address or whatever it is you said you need, but only if I got my job back. If that means you got to go get on your knees and beg the casino manager, so be it. The only way I'll help."

Lingering silence and then Ray said, "Okay, I can do that."

Lance choked a response. "What you mean, you can do that? You're not gonna… How you gonna get my job back. I was just screwin' with you. How you think you are gonna get my job back? Ray, you still there?"

CHAPTER 21

Frank sat in the Sisters of Perpetual Care Hospital emergency room in Cougar Falls, holding his smashed hand that throbbed like a bullfrog in heat. His face was oozing pus through the cracks of Maria's secret potion that had dried into purple plaster patches. The eye that had swollen shut seeped yellow junk down one cheek, adding to the collage of infectious misery. The emergency room was crowded but the sea of sickness and injury parted when Frank entered and he sat by himself in the corner under the sign declaring guaranteed service within thirty minutes of arrival. His wait had now been an hour and forty-five minutes, listening to babies crying and children retching.

The intercom announced: "Mr. Salucci, please go to examining room number four."

Frank found the room and waited another twenty minutes before an aide, dressed in scrubs with a smiley face print design, threw back the curtain and started to greet Frank. "I'm here to take your temp...oh my goodness, that's a nasty rash."

Frank wanted to thrash her with his one remaining good hand but withheld the urge and sank further into the exam chair. "It's poison ivy."

She leaned closer. "Doesn't look like poison ivy."

"You a doctor?"

"Well, no, I'm an CNA, certified nurse's assistant."

"Then, I don't care what you think. Go away and find me a doctor."

The aide crossed her pudgy arms. "I have to take your blood pressure and your temperature. That's my job. The doctor won't see you until I give him your vitals."

"Just tell him it's normal, okay. I been waiting in this zoo for over two hours and I don't need some almost a nurse telling me how I feel." Actually, Frank could feel his blood pressure rising by the second and his hand felt as if it could burst and spray blood all over the room.

The aide held her ground but a tear was gathering in her eye.

Frank blew out a sigh in exasperation and held out his arm to be gloved by the pressure gauge.

Ten minutes later, a short, dark-skinned man with a turban on his head threw back the curtain and walked in, holding a clipboard and reading. He looked up and stopped his advance, looked back down at the clipboard, and said, "You seem to have a rash. How do you get it?"

Frank sank back in the chair with a thump. "It's poison ivy. Don't they have poison ivy in India?"

"I don't know what they have in India, I'm from Pakistan, and, it does not look like poison ivy." The doctor pulled on latex gloves with a snap and drew closer to Frank. "What is that smell? Are you having distress?"

"It's the salve. I put some salve on that I was told would help. It didn't."

"What kind of salve?" the doctor asked. "Was it a prescription? It smells a little like camel dung. I was a veterinarian in Pakistan before coming to America. God, I love this country."

Frank's mouth hung open. "You're shitting me."

The doctor laughed. "Yes, I am." He tilted his head to get a better look. "Now, what is it you put on your face?"

"It's kind of a home remedy, but it didn't work, so I need something that will get rid of the poison ivy."

"Oh, I think it got rid of the poison ivy, and I think it burned the first layer of epidermis, maybe beyond repair. You could have severe scarring."

"What are you talking about, scarring?" Frank stood up and turned briskly toward the mirror on the wall, getting close and squinting with his one open eye. "So, *do* something. Give me some pills that will get this shit off my face."

"If we knew what you put on your face, maybe we could suggest something to take it off. Right now, the only thing I can suggest is that you wrap your face in moist bandages. You must keep them moist at all times to allow your skin to absorb and replenish. You can get aloe at the drug store. Mix it with the water you put on the bandages. Other than that, I do not have any quick fix. What is wrong with your hand?"

Frank continued to stare at the mirror in disbelief. "My hand? Oh, a car ran over it. It hurts like hell."

"A car ran over it?" the doctor stammered. "You should have x-rays. I will place the order. It may be a while, they are backed up."

In the mirror, Frank saw images: Ray, Maria, Sheriff Miner, Lou Luchini, all swirling, intermingled with sparks and lightning bolts. "Forget it. I've heard enough." Frank started for the door, bumping the doctor out of the way.

The doctor yelled at Frank's back while he scanned the clipboard, "Don't forget to stop at the front counter, your co-pay is one hundred dollars."

♦ ♦ ♦

Frank drove with determination back to Hinkley, having visions of finding Ray and Maria in Ray's trailer intertwined in conjugal lust and throwing a grenade in the door. Or better yet, tying both of them to Ray's fake totem poles and smearing Maria's magic salve all over them and letting them roast in the mid-day sun.

With each new scenario, he drove a little faster, grinning. His cell phone chirped, bringing him back to reality. "Yeah, Salucci here."

"It's Lou, where are you?"

"On my way back to the casino. Had to go to the doctor."

"I got the Indian thing handled, no help from you by the way. It's all settled. The guy is happy and he is withdrawing his complaint. So, forget about it. You sick or somethin'?"

Forget about it? The only way he would forget about it was when Ray was hauled into the morgue. "I don't get it. What got settled? Nothin's settled. I tol' you I am gonna take care of the guy. Then it will be settled."

"Just forget about it. All he wanted was for his brother, or uncle, or some relative to get put back on the payroll. No-neck fired him and I re-hired him. Simple, so forget about it."

Frank was seeing stars. The countryside was a blur as he rode the centerline of the highway. "I will *not* forget about it! You hear me?" Frank slammed his swollen hand into the dashboard and then loudly groaned from the pain. "You want me to forget about what he did to me? Never."

"Frank, listen to me, you listening to me, Frank? Forget about it, I don't need no more trouble out there. Go back to watchin' for cheats. You want to keep your job, you'll forget about it." Lou disconnected.

Frank's blood pressure caused his head to pound and his swollen hand to throb. His ears had strange ringing as he tried to concentrate and keep the car on the pavement. The ringing grew louder. Then he noticed red flickering interspersed with the sparks and stars he was seeing. He glanced at the rearview mirror and saw the flashing headlights and red and blue strobes of a police car on his rear bumper. For a brief moment he thought about jamming the accelerator to the floor and trying to make it to the reservation but then decided it wasn't worth the hassle. He slowed and pulled into the weeds along the road.

The patrolman took his time, sitting in his car, running the plate of the rental car. Then he slowly exited the patrol car and walked up to Frank's window.

"See your license and registration," the officer asked. Frank turned to look up at the guy. "Whoa, that's a nasty rash you got there."

"It's poison... forget it." Frank wrestled his license out of his wallet with his one good hand and said, "This is a rental, Hertz over in Cougar Falls."

"Any weapons in the car?"

"I'm armed, I run security at the Olatagwa Casino."

"You have a permit?" The officer stepped back a little.

"Yes, I have a permit. You have a permit for yours?"

"You want to step out of the car, Mr. Salucci?"

"What for? What is this, a shake down? That tinhorn sheriff send you out here?" Frank leaned away from the door, reaching for his wallet again to show his unofficial badge from the casino.

The officer pulled his sidearm. "Step out of the car, sir. Keep your hands up where I can see them."

"This is bullshit and you know it."

The officer held his weapon in one hand and with the other pressed the send button on the microphone pinned to his shirt and said, "Twenty-two-seventy, need back-up on traffic stop."

The radio blurted back, "Ten-four, eight minutes to twenty."

"Now, just open the door and step out, turn and place your hands on the top of the car."

Frank leaned forward, rested his head on the steering wheel, and said, "Why don't you just go ahead and shoot me. This day can't get any worse and ending it right now might just be a good thing."

"Just get out of the car, sir. This is all just playing it by the book. As soon as you get out and I know we are clear, you can explain why you were going a hundred miles an hour down the middle of the highway and, who knows, you may have a good reason. Until then, just keep your hands up where I can see them and step out of the car."

The wail of another siren came from off in the distance. Arguing was futile, so he opened the door, waved his hands at the officer, overemphasizing his lack of any hostile weapon, and stepped out. The other patrol car screeched to a halt, siren blaring, and another officer ran to the scene, gun drawn.

Frank looked at the two of them and said, "Be careful you don't shoot each other."

The new officer said, "Got a smart-mouth one, huh, Joe? Wow, that's a nasty rash."

The first officer grabbed Frank's sore hand causing him to wince, and shoved him against the car. "Spread 'em." He frisked Frank and then grabbed his hands again and brought them behind his back and cuffed him with a wire tie.

"You guy's are really getting a kick out of this, aren't you? The sheriff put you up to this? This the way you dish out harassment out here in the sticks?"

"Anything in the car we might not like, Mr. Salucci? Drugs, drug paraphernalia, illegal firearms?" The patrolman bent over and looked in the car.

Frank walked away. "Go ahead and search. The keys are in the ignition. Oh, by the way, I don't know if the sheriff told you, but my hobby is collecting snakes. That's what I been doin' today, collecting timber rattlers. One got me right on the hand this morning. Som bitch hurts like a … Makes your face all swell up too. I got a couple in the trunk there, so be careful." Frank had his rifle with broken scope, camo jump suit, another short-barreled shotgun, and a cross bow in the trunk.

The two officers looked at each other and then at Frank.

The first officer said, "I'll take your word that you don't have anything illegal in the car. Where's your gun and your permit?"

"Gun's in the glove box and the permit's in my wallet along with my badge laying on the seat. You suppose you could take these cuff links off now?"

The officers looked at each other, shrugged, and cut the wire tie, freeing Frank's hands. "Snake 'll do that to you, huh? And make you smell like that?" the second officer asked. "Damn, that's one ugly kisser you got there. You go to the hospital and get the anti-venom?"

"Carry a bottle with me. Drank the whole thing and still got a swollen puss." Frank started for his car. "Well, now that you guys have had your fun, I'll be on my way. Got to get the snakes home before they get smothered in the trunk."

The officer standing next to Frank's car instinctively stepped back away from the trunk. The other officer stood, scratching his chin, looking at the trunk, and said, "Yeah, you better get going, just slow down, huh. Don't want snakes all over the highway." He laughed out loud. "And watch out for that tin-horned sheriff."

The other officer said, "He talkin' about Miner? 'Bout right."

CHAPTER 22

Frank sat at his desk staring at the wall with his one open eye. He had wrapped his head in gauze, covering his swollen eye and leaving holes for his nostrils, mouth, and ears. The rest of his face was covered with the gauze smeared with aloe lotion he had bought at the Super Value. He looked like a stunt double for *The Mummy.* The knock on the door startled him and he yelled, "Go away."

"Mr. Salucci," the receptionist shouted through the door, "there is a representative of the B.I.A. here to see you. I've checked her credentials. I told her you were busy, well, not available, but she said this was too important to wait. Sorry."

"Tell them to contact Chicago."

"Mr. Salucci, my name is Mystique Morning, I need to talk to you, it's important."

"If this is about that Indian's complaint, it's all settled. Call Chicago." Frank tried to adjust the bandage so he could speak plainly.

"Mr. Salucci, I don't think I need to remind you of the consequences if you are trying to delay or avoid answering questions. Do I need to get a subpoena?"

Frank stepped over and threw open the door, sticking his head out, oozy gauze dripping on his shirt. Both women stepped back. The receptionist threw her arm up and covered her eyes as if she were in the line of fire of a death ray, then ran down the hall.

Mystique made a subtle cough, covering her nose, stepped back, straightened her blouse, and asked, "Mr. Salucci?" She looked at his swollen hands. "Wow, that's a nasty rash."

"Just what I need, another lousy opinion. You should go work at the emergency room. I told you, if you are here about the complaint the Indian filed, he withdrew the complaint, so there's nothing to investigate. You don't believe me, call Luchini in Chicago, he'll fill you in." Frank started to close the door.

"Wait," Mystique held the door, "I don't care who did what. There's still an issue with the desecration of the burial ground. The manager told me you are the one that made the decision. What happened to your face?"

"Nothing, I'm trying out for a re-make of *Night Of The Living Dead*. You want information about the project, call Chicago." Frank pulled on the door but Mystique resisted, trying not to get too close to Frank's festered hand wrestling with the door.

"What's with you people, you think you can just do whatever you want? This isn't Las Vegas. The B.I.A. can shut this place down if you don't cooperate."

She lost her grip in the tug-of-war and Frank slammed the door.

♦ ♦ ♦

Ray answered the phone as usual, without any greeting, just silence.

"Ray, are you there? It's Mystique."

More silence and then, "Hi Missy, how you doin' today?"

"You have a really odd way of answering the phone, you know it?"

"Not always someone there I want to talk to."

"Ray, I heard some news today. My boss said you requested to dismiss your complaint, that true?"

Ray gave a slight chuckle. "Yeah, didn't see any reason to push it no more. I made my point."

"What about all the burial-ground stuff; angry spirits of your ancestors; all *that*?"

"They're still angry… See, Missy, white men fear their ancestor's spirit, make them into ghosts or make them out to be some kind of evil monster; make movies about them. They look under their bed every night to make sure Grandpa's ghost isn't going to jump up and grab them. We do not fear our ancestor's spirit. We know they are all around us, in the sun, in the grass, in the water. We also know better than to piss them off."

"So you think the, uh, spirits, are pissed off at the casino people? What do you think the so-called spirits are going to do?"

"Well, that's a good question, Missy. I guess we'll just have to wait and see."

Mystique was silent and then said, "Wait until when?"

"Do you like to fish, Missy? I'm going fishing today."

CHAPTER 23

Lou scanned a long list of names, penciling a checkmark next to anyone who had responded to their invitation. The V.I.P. invitations had special significance and were highlighted on the list, specifying by notation where they were to sit or if they were to give any presentation. He glanced up over the paper and found Joe Rondelo sitting in the overstuffed chair, eyes closed, hands clasped on his protruding stomach, and his mouth open, gasping for breath with each snore.

"No-neck, wake up," Lou snapped.

Rondelo's eyes opened and he shook a little, rousing himself from the slumber. "Uh, yeah, boss. You's want me to get somethin'?"

"This invite we sent to the government guy in the federal building, the one's that's supposed to give the speech. He ain't sent nothin' back. You hear anything?"

"No. You's want me to check on it?"

Lou thought for a second, watching No-neck pick at his nose like a first grader and said, "No, I'll call. You remember the guy's name?"

No-neck's blank stare answered the question.

Lou summoned his secretary to get the number of the office of Alternative Energy Resources and placed the call. He was connected with a recording that gave him the opportunity to choose from a list of names, none of which he recognized so he just guessed.

The assistant to the administrator of the office of Alternative Energy Resources sat with his legs up on the corner of his desk reading the latest *Star* tabloid. He silently questioned the reliability of a story about Madonna giving birth to an alien and then disguising it as a Mexican chiwawa named Fred. His boss, the administrator, was on paid administrative leave due to being charged with several felonies relating to prescription falsification to acquire and distribute pain medication, so phone calls were channeled to his desk.

He had recently been promoted to Assistant Administrator of Alternative Energy Resources, Midwest Region, division of the

Federal Department of Energy. Prior to his promotion, he had worked in the maintenance department of the federal building, responsible for doorstops, hinge maintenance, and installation of stick-on foam insulation, whenever anyone complained of a cold draft.

The phone connected and Lou heard a real voice. "A.E.R., Roger speaking."

"This is Lou Luchini, I need to talk to the guy runs the place."

Roger looked around, smiled, and said, "That's me. What can I do for you?"

"You don't sound like nobody important."

No response.

"Anyway, we sent an invitation for the Olatagwa Casino's big party to dedicate our windmills. Nobody sent nothing back saying they's was coming. What gives?"

Roger glanced at the big pile of unopened mail in a box next to his desk. "Yeah, an invitation, to a casino. I saw that." He bent over and diligently dug through the pile, throwing unopened mail, looking for the invitation.

"So, you're gonna be there, right?"

"Oh, you betcha. Wouldn't miss it." Roger pulled an envelope from the pile with embossed lettering and smiled.

Lou hung up, stuffed a cigar in his mouth with a satisfying grunt, and made a check mark on the list.

♦ ♦ ♦

The assistant administrator settled into his reclining leather chair and opened the invitation, finding the V.I.P. pass. Roger smiled. The word casino followed by invitation gave him a fuzzy warm feeling like the word birthday followed by presents. He flipped over the envelope and again looked at the addressee.

TO THE PERSONAL ATTENTION OF THE ADMINISTRATOR
OF ALTERNATIVE ENERGY RESOURSES.

He held the invitation out a little and looked at it. It didn't specify his boss's name, just said V.I.P. He smiled, slipped the invitation into his desk drawer without noticing the hand written note from Lou Luchini requesting the administrator to address the gathering with glowing comments about their venture into alternative energy.

Chapter 24

"**I** got what you wanted," Lance said after the phone connected with silence.

"How'd you get it?" Ray finally responded.

"Cost me two hundred bucks and I had to set the guy up with one of the housekeepers and guard the door for his fifteen minutes of joy."

"Hey, you got your job back, so don't bitch," Ray said with a smile.

"Yeah, how'd you do that? You didn't... Nah, you wouldn't do that, would you Ray?"

♦ ♦ ♦

Frank sat in his rental at the entrance to Ray's trailer park, hoping for a bit of luck. He just wanted one opportunity to confront the Indian, forcibly get him into the car, and make him disappear. The disappear part of the plan he hadn't finalized yet, but it would include some payback torture for sure.

Frank still had the mummy-look-alike gauze wrapped around his face and hands and the aloe lotion was starting to dry and cake in clumps. The coffee he had purchased at a drive through had dribbled down his gauze-covered chin onto his shirt. Getting the coffee at the drive through was no easy task, waiting for the three pimply faced kids staring out of the window to get over the shock of his appearance.

A school bus pulled up to the intersection, stopping next to Frank's car, preparing to drop off a group of trailer park kids. The first kid stepped off the bus, looked at Frank through the car window, screamed, and ran back on the bus. Now all of the kids were looking out the bus windows and screaming.

The bus driver stepped off the bus, bent over, and looked in the window at Frank. "Going to a Halloween party? Or are you just some kind of jerk-off weirdo that gets a kick out 'a scarin' kids?"

In Frank's state of rage, he sometimes forgot how ridiculous he looked with the bandages wrapped around his head and no matter how intensely frustrated his facial expression became, it was indistinguishable to the interrogator. So he just sighed, put the car in reverse to back around the bus, and without looking, ran into the car stopped behind him.

The bus driver stepped back and surveyed the situation, looking at Frank's bent bumper and the crunched headlight of the other car, and said, "Guess we better get the law out here." He pulled out his phone and placed the call.

Frank stared straight ahead, his bandaged hands on the steering wheel. There was no way for him to escape without running over several pedestrians who had now gathered from the trailer park, so he sat stoic, almost immune to the commotion around him.

Murt Featherstone stepped out of her car, adjusted her flowered dress that was giving her a serious wedgie, and walked up to Frank's window. She carried her two hundred pounds on a short body and was recognized locally for having gone three rounds with the Flying Ristocoffs' Traveling Circus's wrestling bear, and won. She was especially proud of her 1968 Chevrolet Biscayne four door that now had a bent chrome bumper and a smashed headlight.

"Hey, Murt," the bus driver said.

"Hey, Marv." Murt peered into the window at Frank's wrapped head. "Jesus, Joseph, and Mary, what is that?"

"Not sure," Marv replied. "Could be a costume, I suppose. Don't look real though." Marv turned to the bus-load of kindergartners and yelled, "Quiet down in there."

An electronic blurt from the sheriff's S.U.V. announced his arrival. He stopped crossways in the middle of the street next to the school bus, blocking all lanes, stepped out of the vehicle, adjusted his Stetson, smoothed the crease in his chinos, looked around assessing the situation and slowly walked toward Marv and Murt.

"Okay, Marv, you first. What's goin' on here. Ain't you supposed to be deliverin' those kids?" Sheriff Miner smiled and waved at the kids looking out the bus windows and they all cheered in delight and waved back.

"Well, see, Reg, this here …," Marv bent over to get a better look at Frank, "this here fella, I think, was parked right here where I drop off the trailer park kids every day at 2:48. It's my eighth stop. Last stop was—"

"Okay Marv, I don't need your whole route." Miner bent over to look in at Frank. "Holy cheese and crackers, what the he-ell is that?" The sheriff took a small step back away from the car.

Murt said, "Some kind of pervert, I'd say."

Marv continued, "Well, the first kid got off the bus and saw… it… sittin' there and ran back on the bus. Weren't none of 'em getting off after that, so I came down outa the bus here to see what all the ruckus was."

"Damn pervert's what I think," Murt threw in.

"So's anyway, I tell him to move on so's the kids can get off the bus without bein' scare't half to death and I can gets back on schedule and…" Marv bent over again and looked in at Frank, "and it, or him backs up and hits Murt's car whils't she's waiting for the traffic to move."

"You want me to haul him out'a that car, Sheriff?" Murt asked, pulling at her flowered dress to make herself more agile.

Miner bent over to get another look. "That some kind of costume or something? You look like some kind of mummy. What the hell you doin', out here scarin' these kids?"

Frank finally turned and looked at the sheriff, his one good eye burning from the aloe lotion leaking down his face. "It's Frank, Frank Salucci, Sheriff. This ain't a costume, it's bandages for the burns on my face. Now, if you and everyone else will just get out of my way, I'll get out of here and you all can continue your friendly chit-chat."

"Frank, that you? Frank the Indian fighter? Well, I'll be damned. Marv, meet Frank the Indian fighter. He and Ray Lightfeather been goin' at it for, what, Frank, a couple months now." Now all three were kind of hunched over, looking in a Frank. Miner continued, "Look's like Ray's winnin', huh Frank?"

Frank saw sparks and fireballs and his blood pressure pushed the needle past the red zone. Between gritted teeth Frank said, "Sheriff, you gonna let me get out'a here or what?"

Murt said, "Still think he's some kind of pervert. You gonna just let him leave, Sheriff?" She turned and looked at her smashed headlight. "Looky what he did to my Biscayne, poor baby. You know what it's like trying to find parts for that?"

"By the way, Frank, I talked to Ray and he said your feud was all settled." Miner laughed and said to Marv, "He kind of thinks he's like Custer, no matter how many arrows you got stuck in ya, you just keep shootin'."

Frank had the sawed-off shotgun under the seat and was tempted to pull it out and cut Miner in half, but then thought about the kids and other unfathomable consequences and stifled the urge.

"That what you were doin' here, Frank," the sheriff continued, "looking for Ray? I've heard of using a disguise on a stakeout, but come on, Frank, that's a little over the top."

Horns started to honk as the modest Hinkley traffic backed up in both directions. The crowd of trailer occupants dispersed, seeing there was no blood or apparent impending fisticuffs, and the kids in the bus were having a food fight with the left-overs from their lunch boxes.

Miner rose up from the car and looked around. "Oh well, Frank, what's it gonna be? Can't be sittin' out here in the middle of the street all day. Looks like you got some damage that needs to be cleaned up here." He turned to Murt. "What do you think, Murt? What's it gonna take to clean this up?"

"I think you give me about ten minutes with that pervert and he won't be botherin' no more kids around here." Murt had her hands on her wide hips, ready to pounce.

"No, I mean about your car. How much damage you think he done?"

Murt glanced at her smashed headlight and bent bumper. "'Bout a thousand, I suspect."

Frank tried to turn and look at the Biscayne, stretching some of the gauze out of his good eye to get a better look. "That whole piece of junk isn't worth a thousand."

Murt took a step forward, reaching for Frank's door handle.

Miner stopped her and said, "Now calm down, Murt, he don't need no more injuries. Besides, you might catch whatever he's got."

The sheriff bent down and firmly said, "I'd say you got yourself into somewhat of a pickle here, Frank. Now, I can have Joe Simms come over here and tow your car to the impound yard and write you up for, oh, how about reckless operation; or maybe impersonating a mummy, or something like that. Or, you could just pay Murt here for her pain and suffering and havin' to look at that crunched headlight every time she walks out to the garage and get this whole ordeal over with."

His pulse pumped against the bandages. His head was spinning and a siren buzzed in his ears. He had to get away from these people or he was going to do something he would regret for a really long time, like life in the penitentiary. Finally, he reached into his pocket and pulled out a wad of bills. He had no idea how many hundreds were there, so he just threw them at Murt and they floated down onto the ground like fall leaves.

Murt scrambled to pick them up.

Frank growled at Sheriff Miner, "Now, get out of my way." He put the car in gear and the remaining trailer park people parted, giving Frank clearance to pull up over the curb and leave the scene.

Miner yelled as Frank drove away, "Don't go away mad, Frank, just go away."

Murt counted the cash and said, "There's only eight hundred and twenty three bucks here. He screwed me out of more than a hundred."

Miner turned and said, "It's probably the best screwin' you ever had, I'm sure of that," and walked back to his S.U.V.

Chapter 25

Ray, Mystique, and Nub sat on plastic buckets on the bank of the Olatagwa River, three fishing poles pointing toward the tranquil water. No one had spoken for a long time, absorbing the sounds of the many river inhabitants. Nub had caught two catfish and a sucker, none keepers. Mystique had been bitten by two mosquitoes and been admonished early on by Ray for wearing expensive perfume that attracted the parasites.

Ray finally interrupted the solemnity of the afternoon by asking, "You get invited to the big celebration at the casino?"

"I don't need an invitation," Mystique replied without averting her concentration from the red and white bobber floating in the river.

Nub rose from his bucket and reported, "I got to take a leak." He meandered off into the brush.

"I'll have to admit, that outfit you have on makes you look like one of those fishin' pros on TV," Ray said, plucking a long piece of grass to suck on. Mystique had prepared for their adventure by going to the Wal-Mart and buying a fly-fishing vest with enough pockets to accommodate a full tackle box. She completed the outfit with a designer sweat suit and matching headband.

Mystique took the complement with a mild smile. "I believe in dressing for the occasion, no matter what it is."

"It should be a good show," Ray said, leaning back in grass on his elbows.

"What, the party at the casino? What can they do? I mean, it's not like windmills are exciting or anything. What's exciting about three windmills slowly turning in the breeze?"

"Well, Missy, you never know, now do you?"

"You going to do a rain dance or something?" Mystique asked, looking at Ray.

"Something," Ray replied.

"No one will get hurt, will they?"

Ray smiled. "When the spirits grow restless, no one can predict what will happen." Ray stared off into the distance.

While Nub still tromped loudly through the brush, Mystique leaned over and took Nub's pole and replaced it with her own. She was fishing right next to him all day and had caught nothing but a nasty disposition. There had to be a difference.

"It ain't the pole, Missy," Ray said, never turning his head.

"Then why aren't they biting my worm?" she whined. "Come on, Ray, I want to *catch* something!"

"You need to learn the way of the ancients. If they did not catch, they did not eat. Patience made them successful hunter-gatherers. A hunter may stand silent next to a deer trail for a complete day, waiting for his prey. A woman may stand knee deep, bent over in a cold stream for hours, waiting for a fish to swim between her legs and near her grasp or within reach of her sharpened spear… You ever been to Hollywood?"

"Where? What's that have to do with catching fish?"

"Hollywood, seen *The Price Is Right*, I mean in person?"

Mystique moved the end of her pole up and down, and whispered, "Here fishy, here fishy." And then said, "Is that like a game show? Wait, I know, the gray haired guy."

"Used to be. Now it's Drew Carey. I'm going to Hollywood to be on *The Price Is Right*. I'm going to win the showcase." Ray pulled the grass out of his mouth and flipped it away. "It'd be nice if you were in the audience and would come up on stage when I won."

Nub walked up to his bucket, examined the pole without touching, and then looked at the pole Mystique was holding. "It don't matter which pole you got, it's how you hold it." He sat back down, reeled in his line, and fooled with the bait. At the last second he turned away from Mystique.

Mystique jumped up, tackling Nub off his bucket. "What do you have in your hand?"

Nub hid something against his chest. "Ain't nothin', get off me." They both were laughing. Finally, Nub got out of her grasp, lying in the weeds. "It's some special scent I put on my bait. It kind of helps attract the fish."

"Why you little…" Mystique stood up with her hands on her hips, turning to Ray. "You know he was cheating?"

Ray said, "That ain't cheating, it's just using what you have to your own advantage."

"So you two would let me sit there all day and not catch a thing while this little cheater takes home a bucket full of fish." Mystique turned to Nub. "Where'd you get that stuff?"

Nub looked down, afraid to look at Mystique, glanced at Ray who wore a big smile and said, "Ray gave it to me."

Mystique, still standing at attention, bunched her lips in a frown, holding back her smile. "Stupid Indian."

♦ ♦ ♦

The door valet of the Chicago high rise spoke on the wall phone in the glass foyer. "Miss Morning, there is a… a man… He says his name is…" The valet looked at Ray, sizing him up again. "His name is Lightfeather." The valet cupped his hand around the phone. "Big tall guy, he looks Indian, you know? I mean like, cowboy Indian. You want me to tell him to hit the trail?" he asked with a chuckle.

"Send him up," Mystique replied. "He's…" she hesitated for a second, "He's a relative. Will be staying for the weekend. You won't have to call again."

The valet looked at the handset like he was still trying to comprehend the request, looked at Ray again, hung up the phone and with apparent reservation, held the door open. "Apartment twenty-o-seven. Wipe your feet."

Ray looked down at his ostrich boots that appeared pretty clean, gave the valet a glare, tipped his Stetson in less than enthusiastic thanks and headed for the elevator.

CHPATER 26

Wind Set To Blow At Casino

The Olatagwa Casino plans a gala event to unveil their new power-generating wind turbines this Saturday. The public is invited with the festivities to commence at noon. An address by the Administrator of Alternative Energy Resources from the Federal Department of Energy will be given along with comments from a representative of the Governor's office. An award will be presented to the casino management for their conservation efforts. In addition, numerous local dignitaries will be in attendance. Special prize drawings will be made all day for those who attend. The grand prize of a $1000 player coupon will be awarded at the end of the ceremony.

Three electric power-generating wind turbines have been erected on reservation land adjacent to the casino building on what was once considered sacred burial ground by the Olatagwa Tribe. The casino received a special variance to construct the windmills on the burial ground from the Bureau of Indian Affairs, stated Lou Luchini, CEO of the Olatagwa Casino. Chief Abraham Morningstar, head of the Olatagwa Tribe Council, was unavailable for comment, currently attending a conference in Miami.

The wind turbines were erected at a cost of more than $800,000, according to a source at the casino. They will be operated and maintained by a California management firm and leased from Little Hair Leasing LTD, a firm owned by the CEO of the casino.

♦ ♦ ♦

"Mr. Luchini, this is Fred Baker, Floor Security Manager… Uh, we seem to have problem. I'm not sure what's going on, but Frank, Frank Salucci, well, he's really acting strange. He won't come out of

124

his office. He's been in there now for two days. He won't answer his phone. I know he's still in there because when you knock on the door he just says go away."

"He's supposed to be getting everything ready for tomorrow," Lou said with a frown. "He sick or something?"

"I don't know," Fred responded, "Last time I saw him, he was all bandaged up, couldn't even see his face, some kind of rash."

"Go down to his office and tell him I want to talk to him, *now*."

"I'm on my cell, I'll walk down there." Lou could hear commotion as Fred walked down the hall and then Fred yelling, "Frank, you in there? Mr. Luchini wants to talk to you. Here's my phone, open the door."

After a moment the door opened a crack and a dirty, bandaged hand reached out for the phone. Fred stepped back and gave it up. The door slammed shut.

Lou bellowed into the phone, "Who's there? Anybody there? Frank, that you? What's going on down there? You sick or something?"

Someone breathed heavily into the phone and then said, "It ain't over, you understand, it ain't over."

"What? What are you babbling about? Now listen, I want that place ready to go by tonight, you understand? I've talked to every department, and they are all ready. Yours is the only one that seems to be having a problem. Do I need to get a new head of security, Frank?" Lou could still hear the breathing into the phone.

"The Lone Ranger will strike again. It ain't over."

The phone disconnected and all Lou could say was, "What?"

Frank stood holding the phone in his clenched fist, mumbling something about silver bullets. He could hear the guy yelling outside the door.

"Frank, you done? Give me my phone. Frank, my phone, hand it out."

Frank lay the phone on his desk, pulled a hammer out of a drawer, and drew a bead.

CHAPTER 27

The front lawn of the casino looked like a roadside souvenir stand. Ten thousand whirly gigs on sticks had been planted in the grass, all twirling in the stiff breeze. The billboard-size-L.E.D. screen attached to the front of the casino building scrolled through the itinerary of the afternoon's events while occasionally showing the smiling face of a jack-pot winner in action or an advertisement for Geronimo's Grand Buffet housed inside a giant teepee in the atrium of the casino.

The former weed-infested field behind the casino leading to the burial mound, now called the alternative-energy equipment site, had been sod with Kentucky blue grass so the gradual slope from the asphalt drive to the apex of the hill gave the appearance of a well-manicured golf fairway with giant whirly-gigs as the putting-green focal point. A platform had been constructed just in front of the wind turbines with podium and adjacent V.I.P. seating. The surrounding grass lawn had linen-covered cocktail tables and padded seating for the common guests.

Streaming out from the podium on both sides and surrounding the guest tables were rows of slot machines temporarily moved from the casino building to entertain the growing crowd. Interspersed in the long line of slots were new machines recently requisitioned and designed by Lou and called the *Whirling Propeller of Fortune.* Above the typical digital display on the new slot machine was an L.E.D. display of a giant windmill propeller. When the proper sequence of tiny windmills appeared on the lower part of the machine, the giant propeller would start to spin, determining the jackpot prize, all the while giving an enthusiastic screech of bells, whistles, cheering electronic crowd noise, and fake applause.

The rows of slot machines were already full of players hoping for management generosity through loosening of the percentage of return given the nature of the event. Little did they know, Lou hoped to make up the cost of the event through use of the machines and had instructed No-neck to "Make it work."

Cocktail waitresses with large propellers attached to their backs like angel wings mingled through the growing crowd, offering alternative-energy cocktails, a mixture of Redbull, vodka, and lemon-lime soda with a propeller straw. A bandstand was set up on the pavement near the loading docks and a rock band with an Elton John impersonator hacked at his repertoire of songs.

The crisp autumn day promised to be picture perfect with plenty of sunshine, mild temperatures, and a brisk fall breeze. The local weather forecaster cautioned about high- velocity wind gusts. The trees behind the mound offered a picturesque setting with their fall colors in full throttle and fallen leaves scurrying along the ground.

Lou Luchini and No-neck Rondelo stood near the corner of the casino, taking in the panoramic view of the green lawn leading up to the statue like windmills, their propeller blades locked in place, awaiting the signal to turn. Lou marveled at all of the activity surrounding the V.I.P. platform and the customer-guests inhabiting the slot-machine stools and numerous cocktail tables.

Lou looked at his watch and said, "'Bout eleven o'clock, some of the politicians ought to be showing up pretty soon, hoping to get a handout before everything starts." A brisk gust of wind swirled around the corner of the building, raising a whirlwind of dust. "I hope everything is nailed down, this wind could get nasty."

One of the security guards ushered a tall, thin man wearing an open-collar golf shirt, khaki pants, no socks under his loafers, and trendy horn-rimmed glasses up to Lou and No-neck. The wind blew his manicured hairpiece into a frizzled mess, lifting the edges and exposing the thin spots he hoped to cover. He kept pancaking his hand on top of his head in an effort to keep the mop in place, without much success.

The guard introduced the guest. "This here's Man... Man..." He turned to the guest. "What'd you say your name is?"

He said with a very distinctive Australian brogue, "Manfred Ristoid."

"Yeah, that's it. He's from Austria, works for the windmill company."

"Australia, I'm originally from Lisbon. I wrote the program that controls the turbines. The company sent me as their representative for your celebration. And a fine one it is." Manfred smiled, taking in the view of the growing crowd on the lawn.

"So, what," No-neck said, "you the one that will throw the switch to start these things turning?"

"Ah yes, the preverbal switch. Well, sir, there is no switch; everything is controlled by the mainframe in California. As you requested, the brakes will be released at 12:30 and the blades will begin to slowly turn."

Red Redderson waddled across the paved lot, carrying an alternative energy cocktail in one hand and a ham sandwich retrieved from the V.I.P. concession tent in the other. He sized up Ristoid as he took another gulp of his drink and said, "Red Redderson, Hinkley *Messenger,* I heard you are the brains behind the wind turbines, that right?"

Ristoid placed his hand on his head just in time to prevent his skullcap hairpiece from flapping like a pop-up boxtop. "I am the head computer programmer for Clean Air Systems. I did compose the program that controls these units."

A gust of wind blew several patron's drinks and plates off some of the tables in the foreground and Redderson asked, "I been wondering, it's pretty windy today, I mean the forecast is for wind gusts up to forty mile an hour. How do you control the speed of those things? How do you keep 'em from spinning right off the pole?" Redderson took a big bite of his sandwich and chewed like a cow burping up cud.

Ristoid smiled and straightened himself. "The attitude of the blades is completely controlled by the calculations received from the weather station placed on top of the building. The wind velocity is calculated every three seconds and transmitted via online internet connection to the mainframe in California and then a simultaneous instruction is sent to the computer controlling the units on-site, adjusting the pitch of the blades to compensate for the force. In addition, there are friction brakes that restrict rotation if necessary. There are two distinct machine designs. The thin blades, they look much like an airplane propeller, are used where you have a constant breeze of known velocity. These machines, you will note they have much broader blades, are used where the wind velocity varies. On a light breeze day, the wide blade can catch enough wind to continue to turn. On a day of severe wind velocity, such as today, the computer controls the pitch to keep it from spinning too fast. The units are constructed to withstand one hundred mile an hour winds when the blade pitch goes to near zero."

Redderson, still chewing after taking the last big swallow of his drink, belched into his hand, still looking at the bottom of his glass as if checking for bugs, and asked, "What happens if the computer fails?"

Ristoid gave a distasteful guffaw and looked at Lou and No-neck, shaking his head. "The system is redundant."

"So, you's got a backup system, good thing on a day like this," Redderson said and then yelled to one of the propeller girls walking back to the portable bar, "Hey, honey, how about another," and scurried across the paved lot.

Lou checked his watch as Ristoid followed Redderson toward the bar and noted several of the dignitaries were gathering at the platform near the podium. He turned to No-neck. "You hear form the Department of Energy guy?"

"I called like you axed. The girl in the office said she didn't know his schedule but said she figured he would be here."

Lou stuffed his half-eaten cigar in his mouth and said, "Better be, or you are gonna be giving a speech."

No-neck's cell phone chirped and he answered. After a couple of uh huhs, he turned to Lou. "Security says there's a guy dressed like an injun walking through the casino. He's got a broad with him dressed like a squaw. You hire 'em?"

"I didn't hire nobody. Tell 'em to call Frank, see if he hired anybody."

No-neck spoke into the phone and then responded, "Nobody's seen Frank since yesterday. He ain't answering his phone."

Lou chomped on his cigar and rubbed his forehead. "This is turning into a real monkey fuck. Tell security to find the D.O.E. guy pronto. Page him or something, and tell them to find Frank. This thing is supposed to start in fifteen minutes."

A flock of mallards lifted off the pond in front of the casino and flew in formation over the growing crowd. Lou looked up and said, "I thought I told maintenance to get rid of those things. Just what we need, a bunch of ducks crapping all over everything."

♦ ♦ ♦

Frank squatted in some brush just beyond and behind the burial mound. Most of the lawn receding down to the paved lot was visible from his vantage point. He was nude with the exception of camo boots and the dirty gauze wrapped around his head and hands. He smeared brown boot cream over his torso and legs. Some fresh cut brush strapped to his waist with a belt barely covered his boot cream-colored crotch. More brush was draped over his head and shoulders. Strips of camo cloth taped to his chest completed his effort to blend into the brushy hill. The repaired rifle rested at his side and a pair of binoculars hung around his neck.

In the solitude of his office over the past few days he had begun conversing with himself, carrying on full conversations with a second un-named personality.

"You think he'll show up, Frank?"

"You bet he will. And let's hope he's got the Mex with him too."

"Whatta ya gonna do, Frank, huh, Frank? You gonna shoot 'em, Frank?

"Quiet down, this is what we've been waiting for. We are going to finish it today."

"Yeah, finish it, huh, Frank? We gonna finish it today, Frank?"

♦ ♦ ♦

Sheriff Miner strolled across the lawn toward the V.I.P. seating and approached Harold Hanover who was staring up at the windmills that towered over the crowd.

"I thought you were going to get a piece of this action," Miner said, grabbing his hat before it blew off his head. "Damn, this wind is somethin', ain't it? You gonna be the one to pull those lines off the whirly-gigs to get 'em started?" The lowest of the three giant blades on each unit had a velvet rope hanging down as if keeping the machine from turning.

Harold turned to the Sheriff and squinted, dust getting in his one good eye. "Said there was some big shot from the Department Of Energy here to do that after he gives us a lecture. I'd like to lecture him on what happens to a little town when everything gets bought somewhere's else." Harold turned and surveyed the crowd. "Lots of people; offer free drinks and food and the whole town'll show up. Caught the guy that took all the money yet, *Reg*? Or you too busy keepin' us safe in this little town."

"I'm followin' up on some leads. He'll get caught. He ain't as smart as he thinks he is. Well, smart enough to convince you, I guess." Miner adjusted his hat and looked at his watch. "When's this show get started, I got time to get some of that grub?"

◆　◆　◆

Ray and Mystique slowly walked through the casino, attracting catcalls and whistles, along with a few requests for photos. Ray wore his full-feathered headdress, bare chest with leather leggings and moccasins, red-striped war paint on his cheeks, and a spear with a feathered strap.

Mystique, her hair braided in the same fashion as Ray only with a headband, wore a suede leather sack dress tied at the waste with braided leather and wore moccasins. Her face was painted as well, only with white stripes signifying her unlikely virginity. She carried a beaded pouch with a long leather strap over her shoulder.

As they ambled arm in arm to the side exit of the casino, the public address system requested the representative from The Department of Energy to report to the outside podium for the dedication.

Ray said, "I guess it's time to go see the show."

◆　◆　◆

Lou and No-neck stood in front of the podium scanning the crowd for anyone who looked important enough to be a representative of The Department Of Energy. The wind was whipping and gathering paper plates and plastic cups into swirling tornados on the asphalt and several tables had blown over in the frenzy.

"We got to get this thing started before this wind gets any worse," Lou said, pulling a new cigar from inside his sport coat.

Two propeller girls escorted, or perhaps better described as carried, a guy dressed in plaid Bermuda shorts, a White Sox jersey, and Yankees ball cap through the tables toward the podium.

As they approached, Lou said with disdain, "What do *you* want? Why you dragging that guy out here? Get security and throw him out."

The middle-aged man tried to stand firm between the two propeller girls, copping as much of a feel as he could given the circumstances, and said, "Roger Willowby at your service," he swayed a little and one of the propeller girls steadied him, "assistant to the administer of the office of alternate engerny, middle region." Roger shook his head trying to focus. "These fine ladies, with their twirler things on their backs, said you wanted to see me. I had a machine coughin' up quarters like a cat with hairballs and they made me come out here." Roger rubbed his eyes. "What gives, and it better be important."

Lou stared at Roger in disbelief, his half-eaten cigar flapping in the wind. "Who are you? You're kidding, right?" He looked at No-neck and repeated, "This is some kind of joke, right?"

No-neck grabbed a bunch of Roger's jersey, holding him up straight. "We axed for somebody important, not no jerk off like you. Who's gonna do the speech?"

Roger blinked a couple of times and tried to swallow around No-neck's clinched fist. "I take conception to that remark."

Lou bit the end off his cigar and vigorously chewed. "Get this idiot out of here, somebody call security." He looked at his watch. "We got five minutes to find someone to do the dedication." Lou pointed toward Harold Hanover standing near the podium talking to Sheriff Miner. "Who's that guy up there? He looks half-way intelligent; must be a politician or something."

No-neck squinted to get a look. "Don't know. You's want me to find out?"

◆　◆　◆

Since their last exchange about the windmill scam, the sheriff and Harold had hardly said a word, passing time looking at the crowd and avoiding eye contact. Sheriff Miner scanned the tables looking for recognizable faces, enjoying being the center of attention standing in front of the podium, even though he was not a scheduled speaker. Something caught his eye in the brush beyond the row of slot machines. The brisk wind provided so much movement in the brush and trees that everything seemed awash in motion, but the bare legs sticking out of the bottom of what appeared to be a poorly trimmed bush was hard to miss, and it was walking.

Miner took a slow walk toward the perimeter of the lawn, watching the bush take two steps then stop, take two more steps then stop. As he drew closer, the bush stopped its advance and stood stationary, but Miner could hear it talking.

"Don't go any closer, Frank."

"Shhh, shut up, he'll hear you."

"You gonna shoot 'em, Frank?"

"I told you to be quiet."

Miner got within about ten feet of the bush, now recognizable as poor camouflage, and looked around to see who the bush was talking to. There was clearly no one close enough to hear except him.

"Frank, I think he sees you."

"Shhh, I told you to shut up."

Miner heard the voice, could see the gauze-covered face under the stringy sticks and leaves, as well as the rest of Frank's bare body poking through here and there. "Frank, that you? What the he-ell you doin'? You ain't got a stitch of clothes on, boy." Frank's rifle barrel pointed toward the ground. "You fixin' to shoot somebody, Frank?"

"Don't say nothin', Frank."

Miner looked around again but saw no one. "Who you talkin' to, Frank? You gone loony on me or what?"

The loudspeaker system erupted and Miner turned to see Wally Gypsum, a local on-air personality from WERM-FM, dressed in the station mascot outfit that was supposed to look like a wooly worm, but actually looked more like a rotten banana, standing at the podium and calling the crowd to attention. It wasn't an easy task with the slot machines continuing to sing their electronic loser's ballad and the wind whipping through the trees and around the building.

Miner turned to again talk to Frank and all he saw was a pair of bare legs and an occasional bare bottom humping through brush toward the back of the mound. Frank had dropped the rifle, so Miner picked it up, checked the bolt for an active round, found none, and walked back to the party, shaking his head in wonder.

♦ ♦ ♦

Ray and Mystique stood at the edge of the grass on the pavement observing the unorganized mass of confusion. The noise made it difficult to hear the speaker at the podium and the wind kept blowing off Ray's feather headdress.

"The spirits are angry, I mean really pissed," Ray said, watching the crowd and holding onto his feathers.

Mystique looped Ray's big arm with her own and replied, "You keep saying that like you expect something to happen."

Ray smiled.

♦ ♦ ♦

Wally gave up trying to quiet the crowd and turned to Harold, having trouble seeing through the eyeholes of his costume. "I need a drink, this costume is like wearing a mink coat in the middle of summer. Why don't you just turn those stupid windmills on and let everyone go gamble. The only reason they're out here is to see who wins the grand, and for the free drinks. They don't care about saving energy."

Harold stepped to the microphone, remembering this time to remove his hearing aid, and began, "We're sure glad you all could come out on this fine fall day. We'll soon be dedicating these energy saving-machines behind me and it's only fitting that it happen on a windy day." Lou had advised Harold that after his brief remarks, he should signal Manfred, who was standing in front of the podium, that it was time to start the windmills and the ropes would simultaneously be pulled down and the brakes would be freed, allowing the blades to slowly start to turn.

Somebody in the crowd yelled, "When you gonna draw the damn prize?"

Harold continued, "I don't want to take credit where credit ain't due, but I was the one that inspired the casino managers to invest in this alternative-energy project."

Another person yelled, "Shut your trap, Harold, who cares."

Harold just continued, "These machines are of the finest materials and are designed to last fifty years, producing clean energy."

Another person closer to the front yelled, "What happened to all the money you stole, Harold? Got any left?"

Harold leaned over the podium. "Who said that? It weren't my fault. I didn't have nothing to do with that deal. You hear me?"

Jerry Smithy, School Superintendent, sitting behind the podium, sensed the unrest of the crowd, rose and moved next to Harold. "Harold, you better get this thing going. Just start the damn things so we can get off this stage. We're sitting ducks up here."

Harold, now completely flustered, his glass eye bulging from his heightened blood pressure, turned back to the microphone. "I guess it's time for what you all have been waiting for. Let's start the wind turbines."

The theme from *Rocky* started blasting from the loud speakers and at Ristoid's queue, the ropes were tugged, breaking loose their duct-taped moorings. Nothing happened. A few of the drunker crowd members booed and turned to walk away. Then the slightest movement was noted, and all three windmills started their slow monotonous turn.

After brief applause, Harold turned and asked Father Tom, the local Catholic parish priest, to come forward and bless the event, and in good Catholic tradition, draw the winning numbers.

Father Tom stepped up, coughed twice into the microphone, and said, "First, I would like to thank Mr. Luchini for his generous gift to the parish. We all know how the casino put the kibosh to our bingo-night proceeds, so it was very nice of him to step forward with the nice gift."

The blades were picking up speed and with each pass of the blades, a noticeable whoosh fell over the podium and audience.

Father Tom continued, "May we pray, (whoosh) dear Father, we ask that you bless (whoosh) this event—"

Someone yelled, "Cut the crap, Tom, and draw the numbers."

"That you (whoosh) lead us to be enlightened (whoosh) with your wisdom (whoosh) and give us the (whoosh) strength necessary (whoosh) to meet evil (whoosh) when we (whoosh) see it (whoosh)." Father Tom looked up at the spinning blades and said to Harold, "They (whoosh) supposed (whoosh) to turn (whoosh) that fast (whoosh)?"

Whoosh, whoosh, whoosh. The blades gained speed. Ristoid, who had been smiling like he had on a happy clown mask, stood with his mouth open now, his complexion turning from enthused red to pale white. The blades, they turn too fast. Whoosh, whoosh, whoosh. His cell phone rang, and the dial identified the California control center.

"What? Lost contact, what are you talking about?" Whoosh, Whoosh, Whoosh. "Adjust the pitch, apply the brakes. *Do something!*"

Everyone within one hundred yards could feel the vibration of the towers from the extreme force of the spinning blades.

Whoosh, whoosh, whoosh. They continued gaining speed.

Some mallards that had been resting on the pond in front of the casino rose up and formed a perfect V formation as they flew over the top of the casino building. Their path took them directly into the spinning middle blade.

Thwack, thwack, thwack. Three mallards turned into instant duck mincemeat. Body parts and feathers were thrown everywhere in and around the podium. Harold got hit in the nose by a duck beak. He thought someone threw it from the audience so he picked it up and threw it back at one of the hecklers. That started a throwing match between the podium and the crowd, inclusive of duck parts, drink glasses, and any other unattached projectile.

Jerry Smithy had a large intestine draped across his new sport coat and Ristoid, who was still yelling into the phone, got splattered with a major portion of duck feces.

Those who still remained, hoping to score the grand prize, now turned and ran for the building, picking myriad parts of the splayed mallards off their polo shirts.

Whoosh, whoosh, whoosh, whoosh.

Lou pushed his way through the departing guests like a spawning salmon going up stream, finally reaching Ristoid who was still yelling instructions into the phone while he rubbed duck feces from his face with a handkerchief.

"Ristoid, what's wrong?" Lou yelled over the fan blade noise. "Those things are going to tear themselves apart. You said this couldn't happen!"

Ristoid's face had gown paler and he looked like he might need to vomit. He yelled into Lou's face, "We are having a problem communicating with the controller in the building. I am going to go in and try to manually adjust the rotation." Ristoid hurried toward the building, getting as far away from the spinning blades as possible.

Lou yelled at No-neck, "Follow him, make sure he don't try to leave! If these things break apart, I want him buried under the junk."

Whoosh, whoosh, whoosh, whoosh.

Ray and Mystique walked up behind Lou. Ray said to Lou's back, "Spirit's are angry, make big poison."

Lou turned around, shoved what was left of his cigar in his mouth, sized up the Indian costumes, and waved them off, saying, "You with the worm? He already left. I don't have time for this now. Your checks'll be ready next week. Now, get out of here, the party's over."

"You build tur-bines on sacred ground, make spirits angry." Ray turned and Mystique followed him without comment.

Lou's cell chirped as he mumbled to himself, "Stupid Indian..." Then sternly into the phone, "Yeah."

No-neck reported, "He says he thinks he can get them stopped. Something about brakes, but he says it may do some damage. The thing that trims the blades is stuck. I tol' him, if they break, I break him."

Lou was backing away from the now abandoned stage area as he listened to No-neck. "Tell him to get 'em stopped before they fall over."

A few seconds later, over the whoosh, whoosh, whoosh, Lou could hear metal against metal screeching as the engaging friction brakes worked against the powerful wind. The screeching grew louder and smoke started billowing out of the torpedo like generator cavities behind the blades.

A small crowd of guests stood on the pavement watching the evolving drama. Lou, standing alone in the middle of the lawn, his mouth hanging open and his cigar stub dangling from his lips, stared up as the putrid smoke grew blacker and the fiberglass housings started to melt, dripping stringy long crepe paper like strands of melted plastic down the sides of the towers.

The blades slowed as all the lubricant burned up and the screeching metal fused into one giant molten lump. The drive shaft holding the blades bent from the extreme heat and the blades drooped and finally stopped when they banged against the tower for the last time. They looked like giant wilted daisies growing out of the top of the hill.

Silence enveloped the small crowd standing on the pavement. Then Ray slowly clapped, almost in a chant-like rhythm, and the balance of the crowd started joining in. It ended in a rousing standing ovation.

Father Tom stepped to the front of the crowd next to Ray and Mystique. Lou was slowly walking back toward the building with his head down. Father Tom yelled, "Uh, Mr. Luchini, should I draw for the prize now?"

Lou looked up and gave him the finger.

Father Tom said, "Oh my."

CHAPTER 28

Ray and Mystique sat in their car in the parking lot, silent, contemplating what had just taken place. Sudden commotion at the main entrance to the casino drew their attention, with several people pointing and some holding hands over their mouths laughing.

Next came a bush with bare legs running hard out of the casino with two security guards in hot pursuit. The bush ran across the parking lot, stumbling twice, just beyond the grasp of a young guard who was determined not to give up. The second guard was bent over gasping for breath near the door. The bush made it to the pond and did a full gainer into the lily pads.

Ray put the car in gear and said, "Hope it can swim."

♦ ♦ ♦

Ray and Mystique pulled down the lane to the Letterman farm and parked near the barn. Nub came out of the door and met the two exiting the car.

"Want to go fishing?" Nub asked.

Roger Letterman exited another shed and walked across the yard saying, "How you today, Miss Mystique? Looks like war paint, Ray, who you fixin' to go after today?"

Mystique went over to Nub and put her arm around him and ruffed his curly hair.

Ray responded, "Just got dressed up for the party at the casino. Didn't last long though, they had some problems. You get an invitation?"

Nub was digging at the ground with the toe of his shoe, trying to ignore the conversation.

"Why would they invite me, I ain't never been in the place. It's too hard trying to make a buck raisin' pigs to go give it to a one-armed bandit. What kind of problems they have?"

"Nothin' too serious. A little damage from the wind is all."

EPILOGUE

Nubert Letterman sat in the combination chair-desk in the front row of the classroom, penciling images of stick people in different poses, occasionally glancing up at the clock on the classroom's front wall. He was amazed at how loud the clunk of the minute hand was at each sixty-second interval, given he had spent many hours in this room and never noticed it before. Of course, this was his first detention experience after regular school hours, at least in this room, alone with the exception of Miss Crabtree sitting at her desk plunking away at her laptop.

Every once in while Miss Crabtree would mumble an expletive into the screen, lean back and peak around at Nub, and then return to her typing.

Nub raised his hand but she did not notice, so he raised his voice. "Ma'am, uh, Miss Crabtree?"

Crabtree peered around the computer screen. "What is it *Nubert*? You still have twenty minutes."

"I need to use the restroom."

Crabtree raised an eyebrow. "This isn't one of your tricks, is it, Nub? If you don't come back, it will be the paddle for sure, you understand?"

"Yes ma'am, " Nub replied, resting his pencil. He really didn't have to use the restroom, but then could at least wander around in the hall for a few minutes, un-doing some of the boredom of his penal internment in the classroom. Nub had been assigned the task of writing a five hundred-word paper on the historical significance of the Louisiana Purchase, the chapter they were currently studying in American history. Nub found the assignment tedious at best, and generally a waste of time so he scanned the page out of the history textbook and turned that in as his paper.

Miss Crabtree found the homework assignment to be incomplete and promptly gave Nub an F and inflicted one hour of detention to be served after school.

Nub started for the door to the hall just as Miss Crabtree was smashing her keyboard with her index finger.

Nub stopped and said, "Is there a problem with your laptop?"

Miss Crabtree, not one to enter into direct casual conversation with an eleven-year-old, especially her students, responded, "I thought you were going to the restroom." Then sighed and said, "My computer is slow today." She looked at her watch and tilted her head in his direction. "Don't be dilly-dallying out in the hall."

"If you want me to, I could check the laptop, see if there are any viruses, maybe clean up the unused registries. It might speed it up."

Miss Crabtree stared at Nub, glanced at the clock, sighed, and said, "Okay."

Nub took Miss Crabtree's seat and tapped a few keys and said, "I have to reboot so this will take a few minutes."

Miss Crabtree stood behind Nub with her arms crossed, acting like a test prompter, tapping her toe.

The laptop ended the startup mode and at the prompt, Nub tapped in the sequence necessary to gain access to the school's secret proprietary Internet connection, something he had done a thousand times at home.

"Nuuuub," she said, "how did you know the password for the Internet access?"

Nub gulped. "I'm going to down-load a program that will run maintenance on your hard-drive. It'll take a few minutes." Nub typed a few strokes, hit the enter button, and jumped out of the seat. "Boy, I really have to go, I'll be right back."

"Nubert, you stand right there." Crabtree looked at her computer, the program scanning so fast she could not read the script, dropped her arms and folded her hands, then said, "You think this is going to work, I mean, make it work faster?"

Nub exhaled for the first time in over a minute. "It should, I mean, you should be able to download stuff a lot faster. If you want, I can install some security. You ever looked at Worldview.com? It has the headlines from every major newspaper in the world. You want me to set it up in your favorites? I found this site that has …"

Miss Crabtree listened in calm amazement. Then she reached down and ruffled his bushy hair and smiled, pulling up a chair.

♦　♦　♦

Lou Luchini picked up the phone. "Luchini here."

"Mr. Luchini, this is Inspector Quinn from the FBI office in Peoria. We have completed our investigation concerning the alleged attack on your computer system."

"What do you mean *alleged*? Over a million dollars in damage and I'm still counting. What's alleged about that?"

"I'm not questioning or investigating the amount of damage, I'm trying to determine how it happened and who was involved," Quinn continued. "Our investigation has revealed the origin of the attack was a MacDonald's restaurant in Cougar Falls."

"What, you're gonna blame Ronald MacDonald?"

"No, what I'm suggesting is that the person or persons involved used a public Internet access at the restaurant and from there conducted their conspiracy."

Lou shoved another cigar in his mouth as his patience grew thinner. "You mean any schmuck can just walk in off the street and order a hamburger and, oh by the way, connect me with the casino's computer system so I can destroy the place. That what you're saying?"

"No, Mr. Luchini, the restaurant merely acted as a launching point. It's a common practice so there is no home footprint. But, like most bumbling wanna-be terrorists, they forget that every computer has its own footprint,"

"So, you know who did it? Give me the name." Lou had a pen out and was pressing the ballpoint on the paper so hard it broke.

"Well, no, we don't have a specific suspect, yet."

"Suspect, schmuspect, just give the name of the person that owns the computer."

Quinn hesitated and then said, "Well, it was a government-owned laptop. It was reported stolen a few days before the alleged incident."

Lou threw the broken pen across the room. "There's nothing alleged about this, you moron! You want alleged? I'll give you alleged. I'm alleging that you and your whole bunch of overpaid bureaucratic stiff shirts couldn't find a toilet paper thief in a one hole shithouse."

Quinn continued un-phased, "We interviewed, let's see, Roger Willowby, Assistant Administrator of the Alternative Energy

Administration office in Chicago." Lou could hear Quinn leafing through pages. "He was in attendance the day of the alleged... the day of the event, and for the most part was unable to substantiate any culpability of his department. He did say the event seemed to lack sufficient organization or security. He did complement the casino on the food and beverage."

Quinn hesitated when Lou didn't respond, so he continued. "We interviewed Mystique Morning, Assistant to the Director of the Bureau of Indian Affairs, Midwest Region, she is the person that the missing laptop had been assigned. She also reported the unit stolen."

Lou perked up. "What's this broad look like?"

"I didn't do the interview so I couldn't describe her. Let's see, she reported the unit was stolen out of her room at a Best Western in Cougar Falls. That would be consistent with the location of the attack. She, as well, was in attendance the day of the event as a representative of the B.I.A. She was also suspect of the lack of organization and lack of security at the event."

Lou located another pen. "I want her address and phone number," he ordered and then softened his tone. "Uh, I just want to call her and thank her for all of her help settling some of the issues during construction."

Quinn flipped a few more pages. "I don't have a current on her. She left the B.I.A. shortly after our interview."

Another pen hit the wall.

Quinn continued, "So, the bottom line is the case is still open. If we come up with anything that sheds suspicion on the case, or that it was anything other than an Internet junior prankster— that's how we refer to kids that spend their time hacking on the Internet— we'll re-examine the case. As of now, that's where it stands. Any questions?"

Lou slammed the phone down without reply.

"Mr. Luchini," the receptionist interrupted on the intercom, "Chad Silverstein from Rock Solid Fire and Casualty is on line two."

Lou punched line two and barked, "Where's my check?"

Silverstein hesitated and then said, "That's what I'm calling about, Mr. Luchini. We have your complete file that you submitted, and the estimate of the damage. I must say, well done, Mr. Luchini, we don't usually get such detail. That picture of the drooping blades with the smoke still pouring out, well, it's quite revealing."

"Yeah, yeah, yeah, great, glad you like it. So, when you sending my check?"

"Well, we have completed our investigation of the alleged vandalism and subsequent fire, as you put it—"

"What's with this alleged crap? What's alleged about that picture?" Lou chewed the last bite of his cigar.

"Well, here's the problem, Mr. Luchini. We have a copy of the FBI's investigation, still open by the way, and it infers there is a potential that this may be a terrorist plot of some sort. There's been a lot in the news lately about terrorists using the Internet to sabotage utilities and such."

"What are you talking about? You've been spending too much time in the john reading tabloids. I just talked to the FBI guy and he said they think it was kids playing on the Internet. Terrorists? What kind of nut job are you?"

Silverstein countered, "Now, Mr. Luchini, let's not get personal, this is business and I'm just doing my job. You may not have a copy of the report, but if you did, and I'd be happy to e-mail you a copy, if you were to look on page 122, paragraph three, the report reads, and I quote, 'Although unlikely, we cannot rule out the potential for terrorist links in use of the Internet to perpetuate this endeavor.' Unquote.

"Now, given this statement, we cannot rule out the terrorism connection. If you refer to your policy… do you have a copy in front of you?"

Silence on the line with exception of Lou's heavy breathing.

"Probably not, but if you did and you were to go to the section titled exclusions, you would find form number EX43598-01/11, Absolute Terrorism Exclusion. It states, and I quote, 'Non-certified Acts of terrorism are excluded unless the insured opts to include terrorism coverage by purchasing coverage through the Federal Terrorism Risk Insurance Act,' unquote. Unfortunately, Mr. Luchini, at the time you completed the purchase of this policy, you signed a Terrorism Coverage Selection form number EX87797-08/09 electing not to purchase the additional coverage. Unfortunate decision, given the cost was only eighty-seven dollars. So, that's the reason we have not mailed any check. Mr. Luchini… Mr. Luchini, you still there? Mr. Luchini?"

Sometime later that afternoon, Lou Luchini was found face down at his desk, a cigar wedged in his mouth and the phone still grasped in his hand, having died from a massive pulmonary embolism in his brain thought to have been caused by elevated blood pressure resulting from stress and other related health issues.

◆　◆　◆

Serene Acres Diverse Psychological Resource Center consisted of three buildings located on twenty acres of pasture-like rolling hills. An arched gateway gave way to a curved-brick lane leading to a gabled portico and large entrance doors. Tranquil music spilled from hidden speakers next to the bubbling fountain in the lobby.

Eight patients walked in single file into room number twelve-A, adjacent to the recreation area, and assembled in chairs arranged in a semi-circle in front of Dr. Ven Kattopollita. Dr. Ven, as everyone called him, studied a clipboard, waiting for the assemblage to come to order, which sometimes took several minutes. The daily session was categorized as therapeutic vocal-stress reduction, an opportunity for each patient to vent any repressed anxiety or offer personal insight into what he or she felt drove their personal psychosis.

Dr. Ven finally looked up and said, "Joe, let's start with you today. What would you like to talk about?"

Joe Bugenstein, a resident for over two years, suffered from a personality imbalance that Dr. Ven described in his notes as disassociative identity disorder. Joe thought he was Henny Youngman reincarnated. He started every effort to speak with, 'Take my wife, please,' and then would break into a routine of bad jokes.

Joe responded to the Dr.'s request by saying, "Take my wife, please. I just came from the cafeteria, I'll tell ya, the food was fit for a king, here king, here king. The doc here gave me six months to live, I told him I can't pay my bill, so he gave me twelve months to live. Then he grabbed me by my wallet and said cough."

Dr. Ven stopped the routine. "Okay, Joe, we've heard all of those jokes before. Anything you want to tell us we haven't already heard, besides another joke?"

Joe responded, "Take my wife, please. No."

Working his way around the semi-circle, Dr. Ven came to Frank Salucci. Frank was dressed only in an adult diaper, with exception of gauze that he still wrapped around his head every morning and a pair of gardening gloves. Up to this session, Frank had refused to speak in front of the group, retaining a contemptuous attitude of superiority, knowing that he was the only person in the room, with exception of Dr. Ven (and he really wasn't sure about him), who was not totally insane.

Dr. Ven asked, "Frank, do you have anything to say to us today? We would really like you to participate. After all, we are all friends here, and we all want to get better."

The group could hear Frank muttering under his bandage, his alter personality speaking, "Frank, don't talk to them, you don't have to."

"Shut up, I know, I know."

"Frank, I'm telling you, they're all nuts."

"I know, I know, shut up."

Frank looked around the room with an indistinguishable smirk, crossed his arms with attitude, finally drew a visual bead on Dr. Ven, and after a long pause said, "I am the walrus, coo coo ca chew, coo coo ca chew."

◆　◆　◆

"Ray Lightfeather, come on down!" Rod Roddy, the stage announcer for *The Price Is Right* brightly spoke into the microphone.

The audience yelled, whistled, and clapped as Ray rose from his seat and pranced down the aisle to the brightly lighted stage.

Ray wore his leather vest over his bare chest, leather leggings with fringe, moccasins, and three turkey feathers sticking out of his braid, held in place by a headband. He painted his face with bold stripes and had a leather braid necklace with breast feathers from a ring-necked pheasant hanging low on his chest.

Drew Carey shook Ray's hand and acted like his hand had been crushed by the act. Ray towered over Drew by almost two feet. Carey looked up at Ray with his wry smile and said, "You either have one fantastic make up artist or you are part Native American Indian, am I right?"

"My mother was Full blood Olatagwa," Ray responded in his high-pitched voice and mild manner.

"You play for the Green Bay Packers or something, you are one big boy. What do you do, Ray?"

"Mostly, I'm retired. I used to act, lived in Hollywood, had parts in over twenty movies and did some TV. I met Clayton Moore and was friends with Jay Silverheels. I had dinner at his house," Ray responded as if he were reading from a script.

Drew Carey did a double take, flapping his elbows. "Really, the original Tonto? Man, what I'd give to sit with Tonto and listen to his stories."

Ray looked into the camera and smiled, his gold incisor glinting from the studio lights.

"Well, Ray, you ready to spin the wheel? What do you say, folks, are we ready for some cowboy and Indian *Price Is Right*?" The audience gave a searing round of applause and yells while Ray and Drew walked across the stage. "Okay, Ray, you know how this works right?"

"Sure, Drew, I watch every day."

"Then you know we are going to be right back after this commercial break." The red light on the camera went out and Drew threw his stage-prop microphone at one of the stagehands, saying to Ray, "I got to use the can so we are taking a twenty minute break." Carey stormed off the stage and Rod Roddy came from behind a curtain to keep the audiences' spirit in the game during the break, telling jokes and handing out prizes to those who were not participating in the show.

Ray stood on the stage wondering what he was supposed to do. He strained to see Mystique in the audience but the bright stage lights were too intense. After a few more minutes the audience was getting restless and finally Drew walked back out and retrieved his microphone.

Carey was adjusting his coat and tie, looking at a mirror off stage and Ray approached, putting his hand on Drew's shoulder to ask if he knew what the showcase prizes were today. Drew spun and stepped away, saying, "Don't touch the star there, Tonto, okay? You go back over to that mark on the floor and stand there until I tell you you can talk, okay?"

The floor manager came over and pushed Ray over to his spot and then said, "We ready to go again, Mr. Carey?"

"Yeah, yeah, okay, where were we? Oh yeah, Tonto junior here is going to spin the wheel. Okay, let's go." Drew adjusted his glasses and gave it his best slouched-shoulder look into the camera.

Ray said, "My name's Ray, it ain't Tonto junior."

Drew pulled the microphone down and waved the floor manager off to cut the tape. "I told you, buddy, I'll tell you when to talk. Now, we're coming out of a break. I'll do the lead in and then you spin. This ain't rocket science, so just shut up until I tell you to get ready."

Ray stood there thinking about all the directors he had dealt with, half of them drunk or stoned, telling him he fell off the horse wrong or he didn't cough enough when he died. Now he had Drew Carey telling him to shut up.

Drew twirled his finger to the floor manager and the applause sign went on again, the red light on the camera lit up, and Drew smiled. "Okay, folks, are you ready for some shoot 'em up cowboy fun, *Price Is Right* style? What about you, Ray, you ready to spin for the showcase?"

Ray looked at Drew and slowly said, "Am I allowed to talk now, Drew?" Carey tried to force his smile, giving Ray a steel glare. Then Ray said, "Drew, how about I shove that microphone so far up your ass it sticks out your ear."

Ray stepped off the stage and up into the audience, found Mystique, and they walked hand in hand out the back exit of the studio into the California sunshine.

Ray said as they strolled toward the bus stop, "Man, that felt good."

THE END

OTHER BOOKS

BY CRAIG SULLIVAN

Hinkley County

First State Bank and Distrust of Hinkley County

BONUS SHORT STORY

THREE CLOWNS AND A DOG

By: Craig Sullivan

Copyright 2010, Craig Sullivan Books

♦ ♦ ♦

Chapter 1

Home Sweet Home

Ahhhhhhh, it's about time. Finally, I can lie down. A couple quick circles to make sure the old tail is straight…… now, drop. Perfect! Face toward the heat vent and tail under the drape for a little security. Man, it doesn't get any better than this.

Ham, put your dog out. He smells like dirty diapers. And he's lying right next to the heat vent blowing the smell all over the house.

Great, just starting to get comfortable and she has to stick her nose into it. (sniff, sniff) Dirty diapers? I don't smell any dirty diapers. I'm a dog for goodness sake. What's she want, Ralph Lauren?

Hon, it's twenty degrees outside. He'll freeze out in the garage tonight. I don't smell anything.

Way to tell her Ham. Tell her big time. Don't quit now. Give her the good 'ol boy routine. I love that one. Man's best friend; the whole nine yards. Here, I'll help. (moan) Look, I'm trying to get up but my arthritis is killing me, see?

Hon, I'll make him sleep in the kitchen on the tile, how's that?

Tile? Sure, you go crawl into your posturepedic and I'm sleeping on cold tile.

Yeah Ham, like he's going to stay in the kitchen after we go upstairs. Forget it. That dog gets better treatment than I do. Next you'll be sleeping with him instead of me. I'm going to bed. You two can just sit in your own stink.

Way to go Ham, we got her. She gave up. Nice job. Now, let's see, where was I? Head toward the vent, tail under the drape.

Okay Buck, you heard her, don't chew nothing up tonight or your butt will be tied to the oak tree in the back yard from now on. I'm going to bed. We's got a big day tomorrow.

Big day? Big day of what? I didn't hear about any big day. What is it, Christmas again? Easter? I hope it's a food holiday. (pant, pant) Okay, he's gone. The whole downstairs to myself as long as that freeking feline doesn't show up. Ahhhh, what a life.

What's that? Kind of tickles. Ouch, ow, ow. A flea, a lousy flea is climbing right up my rear like he owns the joint. It had to be that shaggy cat. Every time she walks by me something bad happens. What a flea-bag......ouch. Let's take a little lookie here. Slowly now, lift the leg but don't lick. It's tempting, but hold back. He's got to cross the bare skin if he wants to get to the mother load. Be patient, he's got to come. Use your keen senses......... I wonder if fleas smell? After hanging around on me a couple of days they'd have to, especially down here. Wait, there he is, the little bugger. Be calm, set the trap. He's coming out of the woods into the bare meadow heading for the watering hole. Wait.....wait....now. (munch, munch, chew, lick, lick) Ahhhhh, that feels good. Don't know if I got him but it was worth the try.

(Meow)

Oh great, not only do I have to put up with an infestation of bloodsuckers, Fluffy the walking hairball is back in town. Why don't you come over here and put that tongue to work on something other than slopping down Fancy Feast. (grrrr) Just a little attitude to let everyone know who's boss of this place.

(hiss, hiss, meow)

Flip that tail one more time you shaggy milk sucker and I'll teach you a lesson in cat etiquette that's not in the cat owner's manual. (grrr, bark, bark) Look at the fat feline run.

Ham, either shut that dog up or you are both outside.

Buck? Shut up or it's the oak tree, and leave Fluffy alone.

Now, where was I? I believe a little snooze time is in order.

♦ ♦ ♦

Chapter 2

Preparing for the Hunt

Buck, here boy, let's go.

What? What's going on? It's still dark outside. Is he going to get the paper or something? I hope this isn't another train the dog to fetch the paper lesson again.

Buck, where are you? Let's go boy. Want to ride in the car?

It's the old 'want to ride in the car' trick. The last time I heard that I ended up with a needle stuck in my butt. What kind of crazy outfit does he have on? He looks like a walking brush pile. Man I need to stretch a little here. I can feel the draft from under the door. It must be freezing out there.

Come on Buck, 'ol buddy, we're gonna be late. Bud and Izzy are waiting for us.

(wag, wag) Might as well act interested. (stretch) Could be a trip to the drive through in the making. Did he say Bud and Izzy? This could

be trouble. I wonder if she knows about this since they are not allowed in the house anymore? That even puts them lower than me.

(meow)

Get away from me you longhaired dust mop. (grrr) And stay away from my bowl.

Buck, leave Fluffy alone and get your butt out here. We're goin' huntin'.

Huntin'? Huntin' what? It's freezing out there. I hope he fixed the heater in that old truck. Of course, he probably doesn't need any heat with all of those leaves glued to his clothes.

Hear that Fluffy, you flea bitten, clawless cousin of a raccoon? I don't hear him invitin' you to go along. It's just me, 'ol Buck-a-roo, and we's goin' huntin'.

Okay Buck, get in and let's get on the road. It will be sun-up soon and the birds will be flying.

Wow, could you turn up the heat a little? Hey there's a drive through, how about a little……breakfast? Too late.

You ready to go get the ducks Buck? Remember all that training? The mallards are flying and the wind is blowing. It doesn't get any better than this. There's Bud and Izzy. Okay boy, you'll have to get in the back.

Back, back of what? It's freezing out there……Don't pull on my collar. You know I don't like to be pulled by my collar. (grrrr) Ouch, ouch, okay, I didn't mean that. Look, can't we work something out here? Look, I'll sit on the floor.

Ham, put your dog in the back, he stinks. Dogs are used to the cold, something about them bein' cold-blooded. I read that someplace. I'll get his mangy rear end out of here.

(grrr)

I thought you said he was trained, and that he doesn't bite. If he don't bite, why are all those white teeth sticking out from under his purple lips?

You ain't seen nothing yet butter breath. Pull my tail one more time and there will be Izzy stuffing all over the highway.

Okay Buck, you stay here while we go in and get some breakfast. He's just excited about his first hunt. He'll calm down once we get into the blind.

You mean I'll be calm while you go in and chow down on a double order. Sure, I'll sit in this cold truck and be your friendly sidekick. (wag, wag) But don't forget, I'm hungry too. I'm a growing boy.....and I'm not blind.

◆　◆　◆

Chapter 3

The Hunt

You guys just watch this, when Buck sees the guns, he goes wild. Look Buck, shotgun...., hunting..., birds. Anyway, he'll get excited when he hears that first shot and sees my ducks flopping in the water.

Water? Did you bring my bowl? I could use a little drink after those home fries. Okay guys, what's next, a little relaxation in the TV room maybe? I've had about enough of this outside stuff. Ready to get back in the truck?

Man, I'm glad I got these new waders. This water is really cold. The blind is just another hundred yards or so. Man, it's perfect out here. You can see your breath, and the ducks are really quacking.

Oh, ow, ow, that waters cold. Quit splashing you guys. Come on, this stuff is really cold on the old hangie downies. Wow, how much farther you say? What's this, a shed in the middle of the swamp? Where's the heater?

Okay Buck, sit down and be quiet. Watch for birds. Remember, we shoot 'em, and you go get 'em.

Ham, he don't look too interested. I thought you said he was trained.

Bud, will you shut up and watch for ducks. He is trained. I trained him myself, just like the TV video showed. He loved chasing that stuffed duck all over the yard.

Man, my butt is cold. Why do I have to sit in this puddle while you guys get chairs? Hey, there's a duck. (bark, bark) Did you see it? There he goes, did you see it?

153

Ham, he scared the ducks away. What kind of duck dog barks at the ducks before you shoot? I told you he was a worthless fleabag when you picked him up at the pound.

Buck, shut up, you're scaring the birds away. Now, wait until we shoot something.

Fat chance of that. Maybe I can lean against this board, just shut my eyes and this nightmare will end.

(bang, bang)

Holy puppy chow, my ears are ringing like a telephone. Another stupid Izzy trick, shooting the gun in the house.

I got him. I got him. Send the dog Ham, before he gets away. I saw him hit the water over there. Ain't he supposed to get the duck? He's just sittin' there.

Go on Buck, go get the duck. Hunt dead boy. Sniff 'em out.

He ain't movin' Ham. He ain't doin' nothin' and my duck's getting' away.

Ouch, ouch, don't grab my collar like that. Don't throw me into…. (gulp, gulp)….. the water. All right already, I'll look for the stupid duck. Jeez, what's everybody getting all upset about? Here ducky, 'ol Buck's got a present for you. Man, it's cold out here. Here ducky, ducky. Ah, there's a patch of dry land. Shake some of this water off and try to warm up. I think there's ice on my tail, serious, I think there is.

(quack)

There he is, just sittin' there. He doesn't even look like that thing Ham threw in the yard, kind of cute, actually. Here ducky, ducky. I bet I can turn around real quick and grab him. Okay, steady….. jump….. (grrrr)……ouch, ouch ….. You biting little swamp starling. Hey, watch the ears there Donald or I'll have to…ouch, ouch. All right, I've had enough, one mouth full of feathers coming up.

Well now Izzy, what do you say now? Here comes 'ol Buck out of the swamp and I believe he's carrying your duck. Good boy Buck. I knew you could do it.

◆　◆　◆

Chapter 4

Home Sweet Home (Again)

Wow, this Orvis six inch thick, extra large, orthopedic, camouflaged, down stuffed bed is heaven. A couple of circles to scope out the most comfortable spot and I'll be in the snooze zone.

Ham, if you ever spend that kind of money on that hound again, I swear, I'm leaving. I mean it, a hundred dollars for a dog bed? Have you lost your marbles? Or is it you are just spending too much time with those two morons you call friends? You like that bed so much, you can just sleep with the dog. (slam)

(grrrr) You aren't sleeping here buster, find your own spot.

Well Buck, it looks like it's just you and me. They say, 'A great day of huntin' is better than a beautiful woman anytime.' Seein' I don't have no beautiful woman, it's like a double, if you know what I mean. Boy, you made me proud today. All that training came together in one big proud moment. Man's best friend, that's for sure.

Let me just close my eyes here and enjoy the comfort this bed was designed for. I wonder what that little red head Irish Setter down the street is doing right now? I think there is room for two in this plushness. Ah man, it doesn't get any better than this.

THE END